The

Natural History

of

Sensibility

The Natural History of Sensibility

BY

Louis I. Bredvold

PROFESSOR EMERITUS OF ENGLISH
UNIVERSITY OF MICHIGAN

Detroit   WAYNE STATE UNIVERSITY PRESS   *1962*

Published simultaneously in Canada by
Ambassador Books, Limited, Toronto, Ontario, Canada

Library of Congress Catalog Card Number 62-10322

Grateful acknowledgment is made to the Ford Foundation
for financial assistance in publishing this book.

Preface

The four lectures of this volume were presented at Wayne State University under the auspices of the Department of English in March and April 1960. They are printed substantially as they were delivered, and any merit they may have must be rather in the particular point of view from which the subject is considered than in any pretense to scholarly thoroughness. It is a pleasure to recall the kindness and hospitality which was shown me by the faculty and students during my visits to Wayne State University.

L. I. B.

August 10, 1961

Contents

1

The Ethics of Feeling

SOME explanation may be called for, at the outset, of the scientific presumption in the title of these discourses, promising to present a "natural history" of such a thing as sensibility.

Humanists have not infrequently cherished the idea of introducing, in some way or other, more rigorous and scientific methods into their studies. It is surely permissible to make trial of such methods as attempts towards scientific objectivity and accuracy in our historical and critical scholarship. But we must at the same time appreciate our peculiar difficulties and not defeat our purposes by a vaulting ambition. We are dealing with human nature, and all scientific study of living things has so far fallen short of mathematical certitude. In the eighteenth century the great French mathematician D'Alembert, writing in the spirit of the Parisian group of the Encyclopedists, daringly declared that "Locke reduced metaphysics to what it ought to be in fact, the experimental physics of the human soul." His phrase is intriguing, but Locke's psychology has long ago lost this high scientific authority. In our modern psychological laboratories the exclusive aim of investigation appears to be only the experimental physics of the nervous system, and even the existence of the human soul cannot be professionally admitted. For a workable scientific analogy the

3

humanist must look elsewhere. He may recall that in the nineteenth century Zola boldly attempted to study all aspects of human nature by creating what he called the "experimental novel," using fiction as a laboratory science for the study of human behavior. Unfortunately, Zola failed to recognize the distinction that the scientist in his laboratory works with processes of nature not of his own making, whereas the novelist himself creates his characters and himself determines the conclusion to which his experiment shall lead. Zola's theory is accordingly now long forgotten. Perhaps there is greater promise in the historical method, especially as history is now classified as one of the social sciences. The student of history does not create his material, as the novelist does; he finds it, and assembles it in somewhat the same way as the experts restore a wrecked airplane. As he traces the patterns of historical development, he is observing, as if in a laboratory vast in time and space, what are the characteristic reactions of human nature; and he can draw, if not scientific laws, at least valuable generalizations which can lead him to wisdom. We are about to study in this way the history of sensibility. But the study of the history of an idea cannot, any more than any other study of human activity, be abstracted from human nature in the manner of arithmetic or geometry. The history of ideas is the history of how one idea has suggested another; it is also the study of what human nature has done to ideas, and, just as important, what ideas have done to human nature. The history of an idea therefore

4

sometimes appears to be analogous to the life history of living organisms; like plants and animals, ideas flourish best in appropriate environments and climates, and like them ideas reveal their real nature in their growth and evolution. Thus the history of an idea may be also the life history of an idea, and the historian may think of his work as biology or ecology, or, perhaps best of all, as that old-fashioned study called "natural history." Such then, is the modest scientific ambition of this attempt to trace the life history of that complex of ideas and feelings which the eighteenth century called "sensibility," to observe its development and flourishing and fruit, with the expectation that an idea, like a plant, may reveal its real nature by the course of its growth.

It is surely an advance in historiography that we are no longer permitted to describe an age in civilization by a series of static general formulas and stop there. We no longer accept as adequate Matthew Arnold's dictum that the eighteenth century was an age of prose and reason; we are well aware that it was also an age of sentiment and that more tears were probably shed both in literature and in real life in that century than in the nineteenth. When we are told that society was so stable and its stratification so fixed that discontent was psychologically impossible and that the humble folk prayed:

God bless the squire and his relations
And keep us in our proper stations,

we remind ourselves of the immense literature of protest and the political agitation that culminated, most notably, in the French Revolution. Students of history at the present time have a healthy way of regarding every age as heterogeneous, as made up of many various movements of greater or less force and importance, but all together constituting a highly complex and constantly shifting structure. We learn a great deal about the period from the conversations of Dr. Johnson's Club at the Turk's Head, but there is a great deal more to learn, some of which even Boswell, so far as he knew about it, could not without some peril propose for discussion in the presence of the Master. What we call the Age of Johnson was not to his contemporaries the age of Johnson at all, but rather, perhaps, the Age of Rousseau. Besides Johnson there were three other men of great genius in that century who seem to us to tower above their fellows: Swift, Fielding, and Burke. Not one of them dominated his age in anything like the way in which Freud, for instance, dominates ours. If we are to understand the period as a whole,—nay, if we are to understand these four men themselves—we must acquaint ourselves with the many currents and countercurrents and eddies which swirled about them, some of which are, indeed, much more agreeable to the twentieth century than are Swift, Fielding, Johnson and Burke.

The particular development we shall be concerned with might be described as various explorations and experiments in the general field of human happiness. This theme commanded universal interest in the eighteenth century, both among old-fashioned moralists like Dr.

Johnson and among the prophets of the new age, such as Rousseau and Godwin. It was no mere accident that Locke's three basic rights of life, liberty, and property were changed to the rights of life, liberty, and the pursuit of happiness in our Declaration of Independence. There were even those in the eighteenth century who insisted that our right is not only to the pursuit of happiness,—a phrase that does not guarantee success—but to happiness itself; and some of these demanded prompt delivery of goods according to contract. They believed they had a valid claim against society for any infringement on their sacred right to happiness. On the other hand, Rasselas and his sister in Johnson's tale are baffled in their search for the right choice of life and finally decide that there is little happiness to be had in this life. The theme is played with all possible variations throughout the eighteenth century.

There were of course as many miscellaneous recipes for happiness in the eighteenth century as in the twentieth. But in serious and elevated discourse happiness was almost universally associated with virtue,—a word almost obsolete at the present time. Judging from the essays, poems, plays, and treatises of all kinds, the reading public must have had a passion for discussions of virtue. Translations of Cicero's treatise *De Officiis* were reprinted regularly every few years right through the century. The promise of happiness through virtue seemed to be an unavoidable theme, not only to preachers and philosophers, but to novelists, poets, and dramatists as well. As might be expected, the general terms used in this discussion suffered a good deal of mutation with the passage of time; they acquired new associations and new meanings, and they can be found incorporated in philosophies diametrically opposed to one another. Sharp differences of opinion existed as to the real nature of both virtue and happiness. These differences were in general developed by the great philosophical drift called by historians the Enlightenment.

Old ideas were being challenged by the new spirit abroad, and the idea of virtue along with the rest. In the seventeenth century it was still quite orthodox to believe that the life of a good man must be a continual warfare of his soul against the world, the flesh, and the devil. The good man understood that he was sinful and depraved, and that he had to guard even against the treachery of his own heart. Virtue like holiness required a victory in this struggle, not to be won without some suppression of one's own nature. The moral life was therefore always regarded as a rigorous discipline against the grain. But already in the seventeenth century there were dissidents who objected to these sour views of the total depravity of man. The theological and philosophical controversies that ensued we must not enter. For convenience we may choose to glance at the Cambridge Platonists, those gentle and modest divines whose gracious charitableness and humanity are a refreshment to the weary scholar who comes upon them. They had pleasant things to say about both virtue and human nature. As good Anglicans they did not deny that man is sinful and in a fallen state, but they insisted that he still retains something of the image of God in which he was made. Benjamin Whichcote says in one of his sermons that "Nothing is more certainly true than that all Vice is unnatural, and contrary to the nature of Man. All that we call Sin, which is naught and contrary to the Reason of Things, is destructive of Human Nature; and a Man forceth himself when he doth it." In another place he says that "a depraved and vicious Mind is as really the Sickness and Deformity thereof, as any foul and loathsome disease is to the body." "The good Man," we read further, "is an Instrument in Tune; Excite a good Man, give him an Occasion, you shall have from him savoury Speeches out of his Mouth, and good Actions in his Life."[1] However, we must not misunderstand this kind of tolerance in the Cambridge Platonists; they were not moral relativists; they were not saying that man is the measure of all things. They were profoundly convinced that the moral law is eternal and immutable, that goodness is an attribute of God and must be forever the same. What they emphasized is that the nature of man, even though sinful, shares in some degree the Divine Nature. They quoted Scripture to support this belief, as when Culverwell expounded Proverbs, 20:27, "The understanding of a man is the candle of the Lord." They wanted to moderate the Calvinistic doctrine of man's total depravity, and they shunned the sourness of temper which they met in the English Puritanism of their time. Virtue,

9

they believed, is the health of the soul, its natural state of well-being. And therefore, says Henry More, "to attain this perfection in virtue is to attain the most perfect happiness that man's nature is capable of."[2] It is quite erroneous to think of religion and virtue as burdens upon our nature. Whichcote tells us that

> they who are come to any growth in Religion are free spirited in it, and do it with inward satisfaction, pleasure, and content: They harmonize with it; They understand it is in itself best and fit so to do; and that . . . it tends to their Perfection, and will bring them to Happiness.[3]

We frequently find the Cambridge Platonists using such expressions as that goodness is in the "temper" or "complection" of our minds, and that goodness is "not without delight and choice." Obviously, this is not the old-fashioned preaching of asceticism and self-denial.

The Cambridge Platonists were not alone in expounding such ideas; scholars have shown us that other Anglican divines, also, some of them of great prestige and influence, were preaching from the pulpit in much the same spirit. We need not rush to a generalization that we have come here upon a central element in the spirit of the age. But we can safely affirm that the Cambridge Platonists represent an early and influential phase of a long development of ethical theory. It is this development that we shall here attempt to follow. Naturally, this development is too long and too complex to be traced here in detail; but we can observe its inner propulsion and dialectic by examining certain moments or phases in its history. And the second phase, if we may call it that, must be the philosophy of the third Earl of Shaftesbury.

Shaftesbury was an aristocrat by education and temperament as well as by birth. Instead of attending school he was tutored at home under the supervision of John Locke, his grandfather's friend, who prescribed that he should be taught Greek and Latin from infancy. He therefore enjoyed the extraordinary advantage that when he reached his teens he could read the classics of the Ancients as easily as English. He profited from his advantage. He was not only exposed to the best that had been said and thought in the world, but he had the discernment to recognize it as best. He read, reread, and digested Plato, Aristotle, Seneca, Epictetus, and Marcus Aurelius, and it was to those and to the Cambridge Platonists among the Moderns that he all his life continually returned for his inspiration. Somewhere he has said that they who read many books must of necessity read more bad books than good,—an indisputable reflection, but depressing in its truth, especially for the scholar who has to rummage in large libraries. Shaftesbury was not obliged to master a field of learning or search a library for everything written on his subject. He had small regard for university drudges. He was a gentleman philosopher, and his great publication was not a systematic treatise, but a collection of diffuse and informal essays in three elegant volumes published in 1711, with the leisurely title: *Characteristics of Men, Manners, Opinions, Times, etc.*

Shaftesbury was truly an aristocrat, but it is pleasant to be able to show that he was an aristocrat of the spirit and not a vulgar snob. "It belongs to men of slavish principles," he said, "to affect a superiority over the vulgar, and to despise the multitude. The lovers of mankind respect and honor conventions and societies of men." Nevertheless, the true-born gentleman, whatever his technical social status, was the ideal ever present to him, so much so that he would even identify philosophy with gentlemanliness. "To philosophize, in a just signification," he said,

> is but to carry good-breeding a step higher. For the accomplishment of breeding is, to learn whatever is decent in company or beautiful in arts; and the sum of philosophy is to learn what is just in society and beautiful in Nature and the order of the world.
>
> 'Tis not wit merely, but a temper which must form the well-bred man. In the same manner, 'tis not a head merely, but a heart and resolution which must complete the real philosopher.[4]

This mention of the heart is no rhetorical flourish. It brings us at once to the center of Shaftesbury's ethical philosophy. In a letter to his young protégé, Michael Ainsworth, whom he was sending through Oxford, he wrote: "Be persuaded that wisdom is more from the *heart* than from the *head*. *Feel* goodness, and you will see all the things fair and good."[5] Shaftesbury would not call any conduct virtuous which is not our own choice

made in the depths of our nature. The man who is moti-
vated externally, as by fear of the police or the criticism
of his neighbors, or by hope of gaining eternal happiness
in a future life as a just recompense for self-denial in this,
such a man can only be judged prudent or shrewd, not
truly virtuous. The pages of Shaftesbury's writings are
full of repetitions of this distinction. But note the change
in psychology that accompanies his argument, as when
he says that "a man is by nothing so much himself as by
his temper and the character of his passions and affections. If he loses what is manly and worthy there, he is
as much lost to himself as when he loses his memory and
understanding." Are we not here reducing virtue to a
matter of the passions and affections? Shaftesbury pushes
this kind of argument so far that he even seems to main-
tain that a virtuous man, if he is really good, is immune
from temptation. He says that

> A man of thorough good breeding, whatever
> else he be, is incapable of doing a rude or brutal
> action. He never deliberates in this case, or con-
> siders of the matter by prudential rules of self-
> interest and advantage. He acts from his nature,
> in a manner necessarily, and without reflection;
> and if he did not, it were impossible for him to
> answer his character, or be found that truly well-
> bred man on every occasion. 'Tis the same with
> the honest man. He can not deliberate in the case
> of a plain villainy. A "plum" is no temptation to
> him. He likes and loves himself too well to change
> hearts with one of those corrupt miscreants, who

amongst them gave that name to a round sum of money gained by rapine and plunder of the commonwealth.

We observe therefore that our gentleman philosopher must have a conscience, that is, a sense of inherent rightness or wrongness of actions, regardless of profit or loss. But we also observe that having a conscience is not in itself sufficient for virtue. One must desire to do right, and doing right must be desirable. Shaftesbury repeatedly expresses this idea by asserting that the good man is one who has a taste or relish for what is good. "After all," he says,

> it is not merely what we call principle, but a taste that governs men. They may think for certain, "this is right, or that wrong": . . . yet if the savour of things lies cross to honesty; if the fancy be florid and the appetite high towards the subaltern beauties and lower order of worldly symmetries and proportions, the conduct will infallibly turn this latter way.
>
> Even conscience, I fear, such as is owing to religious discipline, will make but a slight figure where this taste is set amiss.

Among the vulgar he thinks the jail and the gallows, the devil and hell, may be effective deterrents. But it is different with the "liberal, polished, and refined part of mankind." The purpose of Shaftesbury was to "advance philosophy (as harsh a subject as it may appear) on the very foundation of what is called agreeable and polite." The virtuous soul has an inward beauty and harmony

and health. There is a beauty in goodness and a goodness
in beauty. Will it not then be found, asks Shaftesbury,
"that what is beautiful is harmonious and proportionable; what is harmonious and proportionable is true; and
what is at once both beautiful and true is, of consequence
agreeable and good?"[6] After such a series of statements
and queries, we may be excused for suspecting that for
Shaftesbury the antithesis of virtue is not sin, but vul-
garity or ill-breeding.

It must be granted, however, that Shaftesbury, like
the Cambridge Platonists, was no relativist. He believed
that there are universal standards for judging both the
good and the beautiful. This we must bear in mind if
we are to do justice to his own philosophy. But this aspect of his thought was not so important in his influence
on others. It was not his insistence on standards that
made Shaftesbury a great name throughout Europe to
the very end of the century, but his psychological explanation of how man may achieve happiness and goodness by harmonizing his affections and impulses, how he
may perfect his nature by attaining an inward beauty
and nobility of taste. And, in fact, Shaftesbury, for all
his great reputation, was neither original nor alone in
discovering this psychology. Something like it has doubtless occurred to men in all ages. But the eighteenth century found it extraordinarily to its liking. Richard Steele,
who may or may not have read Shaftesbury, makes good
use of it in his play *The Conscious Lovers*. Indiana, an
orphaned young girl without means or family connec-

tion, has been receiving generous financial support from an anonymous gentleman. The young friend is Bevil Junior, and she suspects as much. She wants to discuss the case with him and to raise the question whether such generosity must not be just a mask for dishonorable intentions. She tells Bevil that if the anonymous donor is not intending to compromise her honor, he must indeed be a man of uncommon mould. Not at all, retorts Bevil, such disinterested generosity is

> but at best a better taste in experience. . . . He is only one who takes more delight in reflections than in sensations. . . . Why, madam, a greater expense than all this men lay out upon an unnecessary stable of horses. . . . If pleasure be worth purchasing, how great a pleasure is it to him who has a true taste of life to ease an aching heart, to see the human countenance lighted up into smiles of joy, . . .

And so forth. The analogy with Shaftesbury is striking, and Mandeville made no mistake when he associated Steele with Shaftesbury and shot one arrow of criticism at both.

At the present time we are interested in Mandeville mainly because he opposed the philosophy of Shaftesbury at every point. Mandeville belonged to the materialist tradition, and he discarded the virtues without any reservation. They were mere delusions; they were, he said, merely the inventions of politicians, "the political offspring which flattery begot upon pride." His own ethics appear in his famous formula that private vices are public benefits, as they keep up economic prosperity. But we are concerned now particularly with his shrewd and caustic criticism of Shaftesbury. He thought that his Lordship was deluded in his generous enthusiasm over the natural goodness of human nature. No one before had ever fancied that the path of virtue could be so easy. But Shaftesbury, said Mandeville,

> imagines that men without any trouble or vio- lence upon themselves may be naturally virtuous. He seems to require and expect goodness in his species as we do a sweet taste in grapes and China oranges, of which, if any of them are sour, we boldly pronounce that they are not come to that perfection their nature is capable of.[7]

The criticism was malevolent, but incisive and illuminat- ing. We are sure to be reminded of it again and again if we read very many of the hundreds and hundreds of pages of eighteenth century poetry about "virtue's sweet charms," about "mental beauty" and "moral grace," about "the nice concord of a well-tuned mind," the har- mony of the "social affections" and the "social passions," "the bliss no wealth can bribe, no power bestow," or the "moral beauty that charms the heart." Such constant echoing is no accident. For Shaftesbury came to be re- garded as a sort of unofficial official philosopher of the movement of sensibility down to the end of the century. His direct influence was great, but for us it is even more important that he is so representative. In his philosophy we can study those ideas and enthusiasms which pro-

17

vided the inner drive of the great European evolution of thought and feeling which dominated the latter part of the century.

For the purposes of our analysis the most important observation to be made about this philosophy was stated as an objection by Joseph Butler in his *Fifteen Sermons on Human Nature,* published in 1726. Butler argued that even a little introspection will reveal that there must be something more in the constitution of human nature than a mixture of passions, inclinations, and emotions, and that the so-called moral sense must be qualitatively different from other senses in that it is supposed to have a governing power over them. The moral life could hardly attain to any beautiful harmony of soul if it consisted merely in one passion driving out a weaker, as anger driving out cowardice, then sympathy driving out anger, and so on. Virtue can hardly depend on the assumption that our good taste in conduct, our relish for moral beauty, will consistently and at all times be stronger than our less desirable tendencies. The term "moral sense" was intended to designate something like the conscience. But conscience is not an impulse on the same level as other impulses; it is a reflecting and governing principle, claiming superiority over all others. "You cannot form a notion of this faculty," said Butler, "without taking in judgment, direction, superintendency. This is a constituent part of the idea of the conscience, that is, of the faculty itself; and to preside over and govern, from the very constitution and economy of man, belongs to it." And Butler continues with his famous sentence about the conscience: "Had it strength, as it has right; had it power, as it has manifest authority, it would absolutely govern the world." [8]

This is of course the paradox of ethics that if the strength of the conscience were equal to its authority and it absolutely governed the world, all men would be psychological automatons and there would be no moral problem. It is, alas! only too evident that conscience does not govern the world. But Butler insisted that even though the conscience does not dominate, it must retain its authority of dominion, it must be a judgment somehow rational and over-individual, it must not be dissipated into mere feeling or inclination or taste, as with Shaftesbury and his followers.

However, the wave of the future was with Shaftesbury, not with Butler. The idea of the judgment as essential to conscience faded away as the century progressed, not only in the theories about the good, but also in the ethos of popular literature, in drama, fiction, poetry, and the essay. Adam Smith's philosophical contribution to ethics is significantly entitled *The Theory of the Moral Sentiments*. In this work he speaks with what Leslie Stephen calls "copious and rather unctuous eloquence" about "the demigod within the breast—the great judge and arbiter of conduct." And what is the nature of this demigod? It is built up psychologically by means of sympathy,—our feeling for others, our sensitiveness to their opinions of us and our conduct, and our acceptance of their way of scrutinizing the propriety of our actions.

Thus the demigod turns out to be merely seeing ourselves in the mirror of our neighbors' opinions of us.[9] The authority of this demigod may be debatable, but Smith had no doubts about its potency. In 1759 he wrote: "If we saw ourselves in the light in which others see us, or in which they would see us if they knew all, a reformation would generally be unavoidable." It seems that conscience is after all the still small voice that tells us only that someone is watching us. It has been argued rather plausibly[10] that Burns had read this passage in Smith before he wrote:

> Oh, wad some power the giftie gie us
> To see oursel's as others see us!
> It wad frae monie a blunder free us
> And foolish notion.

One cannot refrain from moralizing on the caprice of fortune whereby Adam Smith's demigod within the human breast achieved immortality and a world audience only by its retrieval in a poem "To a Louse." As for the theory that conscience as a guide can be built up out of what our neighbors think of us, we might borrow a caution from Johnson's *Rambler* (No. 28), which suggests realistically that the process might produce more quarrel than it would conscience:

> wheresoever we turn our view, we shall find almost all with whom we converse so nearly as to judge of their sentiments, indulging in more favorable conceptions of their own virtue than they have been able to impress upon others, and con-

gratulating themselves upon degrees of excellence which their fondest admirers cannot allow them to have attained.

Clearly Johnson would have thundered against basing a moral theory on such a situation. We are not surprised that the one time Johnson and Adam Smith met they did not get along very well.

The greatest English philosopher of the century was of course Hume, a lovable bachelor known to his friends as "le bon David." Adam Smith paid him a beautiful tribute: "Upon the whole, I have always considered him, both in his lifetime and since his death, as approaching as nearly to the idea of a perfectly wise and virtuous man as perhaps the nature of human frailty will permit."[11] We should therefore have a special interest in Hume's insights into ethical theory. But we all know that Hume was a thoroughgoing philosophical sceptic; and as he had demonstrated that reason can never show us any connection of one object with another and that all our notions of any such connection, as of cause and effect, are merely due to custom operating on our imagination, he could of course find no other source of morals, either, except in custom. We have a *sense* of virtue, he admitted, but it is not natural to us. Justice, for instance, to which he devotes special attention, is derived from "artifice." It is a term we use to show our approbation of sympathetic and benevolent conduct of men in the society of men. We are just, not because we obey a moral law (which Hume regards as a psychological impossibility), but because we are moved by the passions of sympathy and benevolence. "Our sense of duty," Hume declared, "always follows the common and natural course of our passions."

With these general observations of Hume on ethics in our minds, let us examine a longer passage in which he wants to prove that morality is not an object of reason, because virtue and vice are not matters of fact:

> Take any action allowed to be vicious—wilful murder, for instance. Examine it in all lights, and see if you can find that matter of fact, or real existence which you call *vice*. In which-ever way you take it, you find only certain passions, motives, volitions and thoughts. There is no other matter of fact in the case. The vice entirely escapes you, as long as you consider the object. You never find it, till you turn your reflection into your own breast, and find a sentiment of disapprobation, which arises in you, towards this action. Here is a matter of fact; but 'tis the object of feeling, not of reason. So that when you pronounce any action or character to be vicious, you mean nothing, but that from the constitution of your nature you have a feeling or sentiment of blame from the contemplation of it.

Hume then adds a very interesting explanation of how our natures become thus constituted:

> Vice and virtue, therefore, may be compared to sounds, colors, heat and cold, which, according to modern philosophy, are not qualities in objects, but perceptions in the mind: and this discovery

in morals, like that other in physics, is to be regarded as a considerable advancement of the
speculative sciences.

The final conclusion he draws is that "morality is more
properly felt than judged of."[12] Like Adam Smith, Hume
rested his case on an ethics of feeling.

It is, indeed, remarkable how the philosophers of the
century collaborated to formulate the sentimental psychology of the good man, the man of feeling, the man of
beautiful sentiments. But they were only keeping pace
with the novelists, dramatists, and poets. The drift of
the age was unmistakable. In France we have the grand
phenomenon of Rousseau, who said of himself that he
could look back and identify the very moment when he
"became virtuous, or at least intoxicated with virtue."[13]
He helped to make it an age of such intoxication. Rousseau was, of course, the greatest reformer of the century,
reforming government and society and education, and
naturally also ideas about morality. In *The Profession
of Faith of the Savoyard Vicar* Rousseau expressed eloquently his intoxication with virtue. "Conscience!" cries
the vicar,

> Conscience! divine instinct, immortal and celes-
> tial voice; the certain guide of a being which, ig-
> norant and limited, is yet intelligent and free;
> judge infallible of good and evil, which makes
> man like unto God! thou formeth the excellence of
> the nature of man and the virtue of his actions;
> without thee I feel nothing in myself which can

raise me above the beasts except the melancholy privilege of wandering from error to error with the help of an unruly understanding and an unprincipled reason.

You may ask, is this merely intoxication? Is it not the very doctrine of Joseph Butler, the attitude and spirit of Dr. Johnson himself? The answer must be that it is not; it is merely the ethics of feeling borrowing the phraseology of the philosophy which it is contradicting. For a few pages earlier Rousseau had already carefully and categorically stated that "the acts of the conscience are not judgments, but sentiments." [14] In a note in *La Nouvelle Heloïse*[15] he made the same declaration: "Saint-Preux makes the moral conscience a sentiment and not a judgment, contrary to the definition of the philosophers. But I believe just the same," adds Rousseau for himself, "that their would-be colleague is in the right." Rousseau's conscience, the certain guide and infallible judge, turns out to be, like Adam Smith's demigod within the breast, a complex of feelings, with the idea of a judgment carefully excluded.

We have now examined briefly the central ethical idea of four important representatives of the eighteenth century: Shaftesbury, Adam Smith, Hume, and Rousseau. It would seem justifiable to conclude that the sentimental ethics was a continuous development and that it was basically the same urge however its expression varied from one writer to another. Shaftesbury's gentleman or man of taste, Hume's and Smith's man of sympathy and moral sense, the man of feeling of the novelists and dramatists, Rousseau's child of nature, all belong to the same family, as does also the beautiful soul, *die Schöne Seele*, of the Storm and Stress period in Germany. Finally, a generation arrives which relies on rhapsody to raise it above the Ten Commandments, a generation which, after rejecting the idea of the moral judgment, puts its trust in the impulses of the human organism as the supreme guide to happiness and goodness. Let us hear briefly two of its representatives, Madame de Staël and Schiller. Madame de Staël, high-priestess of the movement in her day, explains in these words how virtue operates in human nature: "virtue thus becomes a spontaneous impulsion, a motive which passes into the blood, and which carries you along irresistibly like the most imperious passions."[16] And Schiller, a man of noble spirit, deservedly revered by the German people, explained that he sought for the truth within his own heart. "The destiny of man," he said, "is not to accomplish isolated moral acts, but to be a moral being. That which is prescribed to him does not consist of virtues, but virtue, and virtue is not anything else 'than an inclination for duty.'" "I prejudge nothing good," he continues,

> nothing good of a man who dares so little trust to the voice of instinct that he is obliged each time to make it appear first before the moral law; he is much more estimable who abandons himself with a certain security to inclination, without having to fear being led astray by her.[17]

Let us conclude with testimony from two influential men nearer to ourselves. Ernst Renan echoes the eighteenth century:

> Morality has been conceived up to the present in a very narrow spirit, an obedience to a law, as an inner struggle between opposite laws. As for me, I declare that when I do good I obey no one, I fight no battle and win no victory. The cultivated man has only to follow the delicious incline of his inner impulses.

And Nietzsche psychologizes exactly in the manner of Hume: "The will to overcome an emotion is ultimately only the will of another or of several other emotions." This reliance on the supreme freedom of our good impulses as an assurance of the salvation of man was perhaps the most important contribution of the movement of sensibility to our modern ways of thinking.

2

Diderot:
the Frustrations of
a Scientific Moralist

NO EMINENT European came nearer to representing the whole complex of the manifold ideas, moods, and aspirations of the eighteenth century than Denis Diderot. He was interested in everything, but especially in the new emancipatory philosophy. As editor for thirty years of the *Encyclopedia* he made that great compendium of the arts and sciences into a sort of periodical organ for disseminating the liberal ideas of the time. As volume after volume was published, it was eagerly awaited all over Europe, and Frederick II of Prussia and the Empress Catherine of Russia were among the subscribers. Experts in all fields of science and industry were enlisted as contributors. But in philosophical articles Diderot endeavored, so far as censorship and public opinion would permit, to incorporate those new ideas and general tendencies which were especially cherished by the circle of his intimate friends in Paris, such as D'Alembert, Holbach, and others. Their basic belief was in an atheistic materialism, and as science is obviously the appropriate method for studying the material world, they expected to renovate the moral and social world of man by a strictly scientific approach to the problems of human nature.

On one side of his nature Diderot was certainly scientific minded. He had an extraordinarily active and fertile intellect. But we can hardly call him a philosopher, even when he writes about philosophy. For his nature had another side which we cannot call either scientific or philosophical. He was an enthusiast, what the Germans call a *schwärmer*, and his vast collected works are a collection of *schwärmerei*. All kinds of ideas, emotions, speculations, and impressions poured out of him, often gushed out, into the mass of books, manuscripts, and letters which he left behind him, and which have been so carefully edited by scholars. In addition to his work on the *Encyclopedia*, in itself a life occupation, he wrote novels, plays, dramatic criticism, art criticism, philosophical dialogs, whimsies, essays and discourses, and whatever else can be put on paper. It was truly a torrential utterance. His genius was uncontrollable, as he was himself happy to confess, for control was in his opinion a mark of mediocrity. Through his writings and the great mass of his letters we can study the man intimately, and we are not infrequently grateful to him for the abundance of his indiscretions. We can observe his ever-changing moods in his daily life as well as in his writings. In his case we have no need of calling in the help of psycho-analysis. Diderot knew exactly what his frustrations were and recorded them with complete candor.

It was this shrewd introspection that made him confess in a letter to his mistress, Sophie Volland: "I get enraged over being entangled by a devil of a philosophy that my mind can not escape from approving, and my heart from denying." Professor Daniel Mornet has re-

marked that this revealing sentence should be the super-
scription of every study of Diderot.[1] It refers to the
difficulty Diderot experienced in being at the same time
a sentimentalist and a scientific materialist. To compli-
cate matters, he felt a real reverence for moral goodness,
for virtue, a reverence which completely baffled his scientific mind, but which could dissolve his sentimental
nature in tears. Diderot shed many a tear over virtue.

For to Diderot, surprising as it may seem, virtue was
always a more important theme even than science. In
the *Encyclopedia* he praised Socrates for seeing that it
is more important to endeavor to make men good than to
make them learned. Government, Diderot always held,
must encourage virtue by rewarding it appropriately, by
bestowing honors upon virtuous men, and by making
such laws as would give an advantage to virtue. The arts
should also come to the assistance of the laws in the interest of virtue. He admired the novels of the Abbé
Prévost and Richardson because they aroused in him a
sympathy for goodness. "The afflictions by which they
soften my heart," he says, "are imaginary, I agree; but
they do soften my heart. Every line of Prévost's novels
stirs in me a movement of concern over the adversities
of virtue and costs me tears."

In his own estimation he was a good man, even an
exceptionally good man, possessed of strong and fervent
moral feeling. Who could be better qualified to write
about morals? And it was in fact this subject, rather
than science, that he regarded as his genuine calling.

"The special aptitude of Horace," he once wrote, "is to make verses, the knack of Trebatius and de Burigny is to study antiquity; *mine* is to *moralise*."[2] He possessed to an extraordinary degree the gift of sensibility, which he regarded as the psychological condition and, indeed, the source of all moral goodness. "Fortunate and happy the man to whom nature has given a sensitive and responsive soul," he wrote to Sophie, and in another letter to her he described minutely the physical accompaniments of the state of ecstasy induced in him by the contemplation of a good man or a good deed:

> Such a sight fills me with sweetness or kindness, kindles in me a heat and an enthusiasm in which life itself, if I had to lose it, would mean nothing to me; then it seems as if my heart were distended even beyond my body, as if it were swimming; a delicious and sudden sensation of I know not what passes over my whole body; I can hardly breathe; it quickens over the whole surface of my body like a shudder; I feel it most of all at the top of my brow, at the roots of my hair; and after that the indications of admiration and pleasure appear in my face mingled with those of joy, and my eyes fill with tears. That's what I am like when I am really interested in a man of virtuous life. [*Voilà ce que je suis quand je m'interesse vraiment à celui qui fait le bien.*]

These phenomena, which Diderot the physiologist observed and recorded with such minuteness, Diderot the moralist of course advanced at the same time as a sort of validation of his authority and competence in the theory of ethics. We should not be surprised to learn from frequent scattered remarks throughout his life that he always aspired to the ambitious and highly responsible task of writing a treatise on the theory and practice of virtue. It would be a glorious achievement to give mankind a definitive treatise on the moral world such as Isaac Newton had done on the physical world. But there were difficulties which made him tremble. In a letter to a friend in Geneva, written probably in 1758, when he was 45 years old, he explained himself rather explicitly:

> Though I have not hesitated to examine myself and acknowledge how much the subject exceeds my powers to deal with it, nevertheless I have not entirely given it up, but I am biding my time. It is by this work that I would like to conclude my career in letters. If I should ever achieve it, it would be prefaced by a discourse the purpose of which will appear to you no less important nor less difficult to accomplish, namely, to convince men that, *everything considered,* they can have no better activity in this world than the practice of virtue. I have already given this some thought, but I have not as yet hit upon anything that I am satisfied with. I tremble when the idea occurs to me that if virtue should not emerge triumphant from the parallel treatment, the result would almost be an apologia for vice.[3]

However, the subject of virtue proved to be so elusive, and the difficulty of hitting upon satisfactory things to say about it proved to be so great, that the parallel treatment never got written and virtue happily escaped from this particular dangerous contest.

For in order to write a treatise on morality one must believe that there is such a subject. Diderot's difficulty began here. It is true that he was an important moral critic of his age and country. Like the other emancipated minds of his circle, he never wearied of tearing the mask off the immoral and hypocritical society around him. All the instincts of his nature, as well as his intellectual candor, made hypocrisy revolting to him. He directed against it the shafts of his brilliant satire. But there is a perplexing ambiguity in Diderot's satire. There are moments when he appears to align himself firmly with moral principles and to satirize the immoral conduct as well as the hypocrisy of his victims; then he is a satirist in the manner of Swift or Erasmus or Juvenal, and the reader can understand and approve. Diderot hated injustice and oppression; he hated all the mental and physical suffering caused by the abuse of established authority or pernicious convention. He was capable of intense moral feeling and indignation.

But the reader has hardly entrusted himself to Diderot's satire when he is disturbed by a change of tone. The righteous indignation pales, a moral levity takes its place, and the satire changes into farcical mockery and hilarious comedy. Some devil of a philosophy intervenes and makes a farce out of the moral principles themselves. Guided by his feelings and instincts Diderot is capable of moral indignation and satire; guided by his philosophy, he is capable only of mockery, mockery even of his own seriousness. This ambivalence of his nature, is, I take it, the simple explanation of that strange dialog, *Rameau's Nephew.*

Diderot was not satisfied merely to attack corruption in church and state, or the French custom of selling daughters in marriage. He wanted to cut much deeper than that; he was always seeking basic principles. He was by conviction a scientific positivist, and for that reason has always interested Marxian philosophers. When he used the current cliché of his time that man should live according to Nature, he meant such a nature as is knowable to science. But he was also a sentimentalist and a great believer in the essential goodness of human nature, and on that premise living according to Nature meant to him the emancipation of the instincts, emotions, and impulses of man from the restrictions of conventional society and traditional morality. In this matter the people of Tahiti seemed to him to have much to teach us. If mankind could only be persuaded to take the first step of distinguishing between conventional man and natural man the whole ethical problem would immediately be clarified. Clearly, then, the most important mission of the ethical philosopher is to popularize this distinction. In the *Supplement* to Bougainville's account of Tahiti, we find a statement of this fundamental problem:

> Would you like to have an epitome of almost all human misery? Here it is. There existed a nat-

ural man; there was brought in from outside of this natural man an artificial man, and in the cavern there has broken out a civil war between them which lasts as long as life. Sometimes the natural man is the stronger, sometimes he is prostrated by the moral and artificial man.

To put an end to this unnecessary civil war within the nature of man was the grand ambition of the naturalistic ethics of the eighteenth century, and the longing for the complete emancipation of the natural man was at the core of the philosophical revolution then capturing the minds of men.

As a commentary on Diderot we may cite a mocking passage by La Mettrie on the two kinds of ethics: "According to the first kind," he says,

man has only to yield to the agreeable impulsions of nature; according to the other, one must stiffen and kick against nature. According to the first, it is sufficient that one conforms to oneself, that one is what one is, and in a way resembles himself; according to the other, one must be like others in spite of himself, live and almost think like others. What a comedy![4]

For our immediate purposes, the important question raised by this kind of thinking is not whether free love is better than monogamy, at least for the males, or whether the children in our schools live a life according to Nature. Our question is: assuming that the statement of the basic problem by Diderot and La Mettrie is correct, how are you going to hit upon anything satisfactory to say in a book on ethics? For if we are to exclude from morality anything that goes against the grain, or as Shaftesbury put it, lies contrary to the savor of things, what morality is left? The moral law, if there is any meaning in the term, can be broken and is constantly being broken. Physical law can of course not be broken by man,—only by divine miracle. Diderot was perfectly aware of such considerations, but he could not do anything with them. In his amusing story about *Jacques le fataliste* he tells how a poor, simple soldier had learned about Spinoza from his captain and how henceforth he applied the one idea of cause and effect to everything he saw and everything that happened. "The distinction between the physical world and the moral world," comments Diderot, "made no sense to the poor noddle of Jacques." But with all respect to Diderot it must be stated that what he says of Jacques is true of himself as well. There is plenty of evidence that Diderot was guilty of the same confusion as poor Jacques.

In the first place, Diderot was committed by his philosophy to reject any ethics not established by a scientific or experimental method. He rejected as a mere chimera the idea of the moral sense advanced in England by Hutcheson, Adam Smith, and others. He preferred to look in the direction of physiology and medicine for a solid foundation of morality. In the second place, Diderot was, for all his sentiment, a thoroughgoing materialist when he turned to philosophical reasoning about human nature. On that point he was in perfect agreement with

37

Holbach, Helvetius, and La Mettrie. In 1772 Holbach published a French translation of Hobbes's little treatise *On Human Nature*. Diderot, who now made his first acquaintance with the work, was transported with it. This little book, he wrote to the Empress Catherine, he would have used as a catechism in bringing up his child, if he could have brought her up as he pleased. In his plan for a Russian university he praised it as the only book he knew which presented the kind of knowledge of human nature, the *connaissance de l'homme*, from which it would be possible to derive a really universal morality, a *morale universelle*. He was delighted with this brief, categorical, lucid exposition of a mechanistic psychology. But how does one proceed from this psychology to write a treatise of universal moral principles? Why should any one exhort a machine to live according to Nature?

As a matter of fact, Diderot did not bother to push his ethical speculation in that direction, except as a mode of attacking what he objected to. He had no faith in any moral guidance from the cosmic process. In a letter to Sophie Volland he remarked that "to tell the truth I believe that Nature is absolutely indifferent to good and evil; She is concerned only with two purposes: the preservation of the individual and the propagation of the species."[5] Such a Nature seems to offer little scope for ethics. In the propagation of the species Nature has needed little assistance from the ethical philosopher. But from Diderot's many scattered remarks we might con-

clude that he hoped to found ethics on the principle of
the preservation of the individual. He sought to relate
morals to biology, physiology, and medicine. More than
once he asserted that medicine and ethics largely over-
lap, as both deal with the conditions of health of the
human organism. Thus Diderot, instructing his daughter
in morals on their afternoon walks, explained to her that
over-indulgence in eating late dinners at night causes
indigestion the next morning. But even when all is said
about this health of the organism, the organism itself
must on Diderot's principles be considered as a mech-
anism, and the distinction between the moral and the
physical world is as meaningless for Diderot as for the
poor noddle of Jacques the Fatalist. The plaguing philosophy that his head could not reject was always turning up.

However, this was also the philosophy that his heart
could not accept. Very often in the life and writings of
Diderot the heart triumphed over the head, but we must
limit ourselves to one rather important such incident.
It so happened that about 1778 a publisher asked Diderot to furnish notes for a projected edition of Seneca.
His rereading of Seneca proved to be nothing less than
a revelation to him; he wished he had experienced this
illuminating discovery at the age of thirty. The moral
elevation of Seneca's *Epistles* and the heroism of his
death stirred to the depths all of Diderot's noble and
generous impulses. It now occurred to him that morals
is a simple and clear science for ignorant people, but the
most obscure and difficult one for the learned. The ordi-

nary man, he said, can sense at once what the philosopher labors long to demonstrate.[6] He turned with anger and indignation on La Mettrie, long since dead, because of his book called *Anti-Seneca, or a Discourse on Happiness.* According to Diderot, this former colleague in philosophical materialism had ignorantly misrepresented Seneca and had introduced misunderstanding and confusion into both morals and philosophy. He was unprincipled, his wit made his mixture of truth and falsehood appeal to the undiscriminating, he reduced happiness (*bonheur*) to nothing but pleasure, he aspersed Seneca's character and misrepresented his ideas, and, above all, in his comment on the death of Seneca, he ridiculed the very idea of martyrdom for truth and righteousness. Diderot was deeply offended. He probed with anguish into the tragic fate of Seneca for a justification of a virtuous life. Where rewards and punishments are so irrationally allotted as to Nero and Seneca, there must be some supreme inward value, some recompensing satisfaction in the heart of the good man. "Can it be true," he cried, "can it be true that Heaven has done enough for Seneca when it made him good, and that Nero was sufficiently punished in that his nature was wicked? *Je le crois, oui, je le crois,* I believe it, yes, I believe it."

There were perhaps some overtones here, some suggestion, for instance, of Richardson and Clarissa Harlowe. Diderot considered Richardson one of the greatest authors and he probably wept more over the fate of Clarissa than over any other character in literature. She also suffered martyrdom for virtue, and thus proved to our hearts that virtue is good intrinsically. In his *Eulogy of Richardson* Diderot had said exactly that: "If it is important that men should be impressed with the fact that, without regard to any future state, the best way to be happy is to be virtuous, what a great service Richardson has done to mankind! He has not proved this truth, but he has made us feel it. In every line he writes, he makes us choose by preference the side of oppressed virtue rather than that of triumphant vice." Diderot felt a moral sublimity in the death of Clarissa just as he did in the death of Seneca.

From one of Diderot's letters to Sophie we learn that this question of martyrdom came up for discussion one day when Holbach, Naigeon, and Diderot were on a picnic. The brilliant and witty Naigeon ridiculed martyrdom and Diderot defended it. "I consulted my heart," he wrote Sophie, "and I found it unshakeable in its conviction." The argument was a merry one, Diderot records: "Never was such an important question treated with more gaiety or less pedantry; we laughed like kids." But Diderot was perturbed and wrote Sophie that he could not reconcile himself to the shameful improbity of Naigeon. "O Naigeon," he wrote, "if your Seneca, if your Epictetus had heard you, what would they have said!"

However, the ever changeable and capricious Diderot did not customarily dwell long on such heights, even when discussing morals. He sometimes asked Sophie for her opinion on cases of conscience. For instance, a wife solicits a promotion for her husband, which the higher official promises on condition that she yield herself to his importunities. Diderot explains that he himself thought that she had a right to yield, that considering what was at stake for her husband and herself and their children some relaxation of censure ought to be permissible in this case, especially as the wife already had one lover in addition to her husband. What does my dear Sophie think? Sophie and her sister seem to have joined in replying with severity, for Diderot in turn defended his own opinions with a vigorous jocularity which must not be quoted here. Another problem: a healthy woman of thirty, who wants children but objects to marriage as slavery, explains her desire to a married man, who asks for a fortnight to consider the matter. What does Sophie think about this? Sophie had some fears that this woman was a fantastic, had a *tête bizarre*. Diderot retorted with some warmth that the woman did not have a *tête bizarre*, that she was a sensible and honorable person. But, we ask, how is this to be reconciled with the sentiment of martyrdom for virtue? We might be tempted to exclaim to Diderot: "If your admired Richardson had read these letters, or,—more to the point,—if Clarissa Harlowe in her tragic situation had read them, what would she have said? How could she have been sustained in her martyrdom by such opinions?"

These whims and vagaries are not only characteristic of Diderot's temperament, but they also indicate some of the difficulties he would have run into had he set about writing the great treatise on morality. Ideas possessed him rather than he them. As Émile Faguet has said, he lived in a state of continual intellectual intoxication. He was irrepressibly *bavard* both in his talk and in his writing. He could pass in a page from elevated dithyramb to hilarious mockery to trembling sensibility. He indulged his own nature to the full, and in his nature there was a large element of the *esprit Gaulois* which might prove highly troublesome in a parallel between the virtues and the vices.

As we gather up fragments from his works to piece together what probably would have been his system of ethics, we discover that the idea of indulging one's own nature was probably his basic concept. He was convinced that the civil war in the heart of man is between natural man and artificial man, and that salvation can come only by the complete emancipation of the natural man. Here he represents his age as truly as Rousseau. Diderot would not accept the moral sense theory of his English contemporaries, but he is in agreement with them in rejecting the ethical judgment; like them he believed that virtue is only an emotional or affective state. He went beyond them in his physiological theorizing, in his conviction that virtue is to be understood only in relation to man conceived as an organism. He never wearied of talking about virtue, but he preferred the word *happiness* (*bonheur*) as more exactly expressive of his idea. Happiness is the healthy state of mind and body. "There is only one duty," he wrote the Empress Catherine, "that of being happy. Because my natural, invincible, inalienable inclination is to be happy, that is the source, and the unique source, of my true duties."[7] In his *Elements of Physiology* he naturally had something to say about morals as a branch of that science. He brings morals closer to the nervous system. "There is only one passion," he observes, "that of being happy. This passion is called by different names, according as it is inspired by different aims; it is vice or virtue depending on its means and consequences."[8] Thus we have a categorical statement, not just that the virtuous life is the happy one, but the somewhat different proposition that the happy life is the virtuous one. It makes some difference in which direction the argument goes. For if the morally good is the health of the human organism, if ethics is a science corollary to physiology, then all moral values are merely statements of the needs or desires of the organism. And surely each individual knows best whether or not he is achieving happiness for himself. As a mere physiological organism a man needs what he thinks he needs and when he thinks he needs it. This line of thought was indeed extremely attractive to Diderot and he frequently developed it with a fertile imagination. He liked to have a full wind and all sails out, and why worry about the rudder? Early in his career, in the *Pensées Philosophiques* of 1746, he was already of this persuasion: "It is only the passions," he wrote, "and the grand passions, that have the power to raise the mind to great things . . . Mediocre passions make commonplace men . . . Slackened or frustrated passions degrade the extraordinary men." But he adds that it is desirable to establish among these strong passions *une juste harmonie,* thus reminding us of the English disciples of Shaftesbury. However, as there is no principle of control either recognizable or permissible, according to this philosophy, Diderot can only suggest a balancing of passions. "Constraint," he says, "destroys the grandeur and energy of nature . . . But if hope is balanced by fear, sense of honor by love of life, inclination to pleasure by concern for health, you would see neither libertines, nor dare-devils nor cowards." Long before he could have read anything by the English philosopher, Diderot arrived at the same psychology as Hume. Both attempted to describe the moral life without including the conscience; both sought to present an ethical theory without giving a place to the moral judgment.

But if the virtues rise so spontaneously out of the recesses of human nature, are men then naturally good? Diderot, along with the whole sentimental movement, answered unequivocally:

Yes, my friend, and very good. Water, air, fire, earth, every thing in nature is good. The tempest which sweeps over us late in autumn and shakes the forests, breaks off the dead branches of the trees; the tempest whips up the waters of the sea and purifies them; the volcano sends out the steam that purifies the air. . . . It is only these miserable conventions that pervert man, and not human nature. In fact, what can move us so deeply as the recital of a generous action? Where is the unfortunate man who can hear coldly the plaint of a good man?

This is standard eighteenth-century eulogy of the natural man, but it is disquieting to have to accept as good even volcanos and tempests. Does Diderot mean that the tempests and volcanos within human nature are also good?

On the whole, Diderot was fairly consistent in believing that they are. This conviction is almost a necessary consequence of the mixture of rhapsody and science in his conception of living according to Nature. He could not believe that there could be anything bad in the release of our natural energies or in the indulgence of our natural inclinations. He was fond of the word *fou* and of talented persons who know how to indulge in folly. Such people are spontaneous, original, individual, and they allow their natural gifts to blossom. Such, for instance, was the nephew of Rameau. This brilliant but depraved parasite shamelessly boasted of his skill and success in all such arts as deception, flattery, and even procuring, and treated all the usual moral values with Mephistophelian mockery. Diderot argues with him, laughs at him, and is shocked by him, in turns. But the nephew defends his every vice as his "moral idiom," to which he is as entitled as any provincial to his own linguistic idiom. And against this argument Diderot really has nothing very satisfactory to say.

Diderot could not but admire the extraordinary person, be he good or bad. He joined in the worship of genius, sublime and free as the eagle in its flight, which became so important a tendency towards the end of the century. He admired the man of many moods, unpredictable, strange, fascinating, mysterious, the Romantic dream of the man of genius. Diderot had his full share of French *esprit*, but he valued much more highly what the Germans called *das dämonische*. In one of his art criticisms he uttered this warning: "Beware of such men as come with pockets full of *esprit* which they strew over all their speech. They are witty, but they are not pursued of the demon; they are neither sad, sombre, melancholy, nor addicted to silences; they are never awkward, never stupid."[9] Diderot was prophetic in his special reverence for what is now called deviant personality, for the wild, the wayward, the suffering, the vicious, even the criminal, man of genius. He explained more than once that a virtuous and respectable Racine would have been a flat mediocrity; but Racine *méchant* went his own way and left us works of enduring value.[10] But how would this have fitted into the parallel of the virtues and vices?

Thus we have pursued Diderot in his devious ways, even as he was pursuing the elusive idea of virtue and exhibiting to us his special gift for the study of ethics. Perhaps this exercise can be accepted as a bit of experimental physics of the human soul, for which Diderot's friend D'Alembert expressed a desire. If it has been a failure in its search for the principle of the good, we may

47

take refuge in the remark made by laboratory scientists that a scientific failure is sometimes as helpful and revealing as a success. For we have seen Diderot working over the same theories and conceptions as his contemporary sentimentalists in England, and, like them, trying to establish moral values without permitting any authority to the moral judgment. We have seen how, when he injected scientific ideas into the experiment, he only confirmed the moral anarchy in which he was floundering. Our experiment must have shown why the great ethical treatise never got written.

But let us give Diderot credit for that deep urge within him to search for eternal truth, for his insuppressible longing for something stable in morality. In one of his dialogs a character speaks for him as follows:

> I behold truth and virtue as two grand statues elevated above the surface of the earth, indestructible in the midst of the ravages and ruins of everything surrounding them. These great figures are sometimes concealed by clouds: then men move only in darkness. . . . But the moment arrives when the clouds open, and men, prostrate in homage, recognize truth and acknowledge virtue. Everything else passes, and virtue and truth alone endure.[11]

Something within Diderot wanted to believe all that. But alas! Diderot had also demonstrated that the only thing eternal is the law of perpetual change which prevents anything from being eternal. Diderot, the emancipated wit, the physiologist, the sentimental apologist for human idiosyncrasies, was all his life demonstrating that such eternal virtue was only an illusion. And therefore Diderot, instead of writing the treatise on ethics, produced the mockery of *Jacques le fataliste* and *Rameau's Nephew*. Jonathan Swift once remarked that a ridiculous tragedy is the worst species of literary composition. Taken as a whole, Diderot's career as a moralist and ethical thinker comes very close to being just that—a ridiculous tragedy.

3

The Exaltation of Unhappiness

*I*N EVERY theory of virtue, and in every conception of happiness, there must be some idea of self-realization, of one sort or another. And the kind of self-realization that is advocated or preferred must depend in the first place on what one conceives the self to be. The ethical regimen that would meet with the approval of such men as Swift or Dr. Johnson would be the very antithesis of the principles of such a man as Rousseau. But every conception of the nature of man does necessarily involve, as corollaries to its principle, thories and programs regarding education, society, manners, government, and the general conduct of life.

We should therefore expect to find in the literature of the eighteenth century the means whereby the man of sensibility might cultivate and develop the harmony and beauty of his nature, the means for raising his soul to perfection. And of course the eighteenth century provided such a literature in abundance. Its themes are as manifold as the modes of sensibility. The drama and the novel presented the pathetic sufferings of the unfortunate, the persecuted, the star-crossed and the victims of evil destiny, and thus taught the softened heart to shed the sympathetic tear. For, as James Thomson observed, it is the prerogative of man over other animals that he alone has been taught to weep.[1] The poets, if we may

believe what they say in their poetry, began to feel a dis-
like for the prosaic level of ordinary society, and to with-
draw into solitude for meditation on a higher level. They
were particularly inclined to wander alone in the woods
and among the hills in the soft hours of evening, "there
to converse with Nature and harmonize the heart." [2] Not
that friends were despised, provided they were "attuned
to happy unison of soul," for friendships of that kind
were an important part of the lives of the men of sensibility. But moments of solitude were absolutely essential to them. At midnight hour they wandered among the
ruined abbey's moss-grown piles and thrilled to the lone
screech-owl's note, and then descended into the charnels
with only the flickering light of a candle casting ghostly
shadows in the cavernous depths. We need not pursue
the catalog of the pleasures revealed to the man of sensibility. The many resources—or shall we call them stimu-
lants?—available to him were rehearsed by all the poets,
and the historian finds them all conveniently collected
in the early poems of Joseph and Thomas Warton.

Thomas Warton gave his poem the title *The Pleasures of Melancholy*. The phrase enjoyed great currency
in the eighteenth century, and in Germany it is translated in Goethe's phrase, *die Wonne der Wehmut*. Melancholy seemed to be essential to the make-up of the
man of sensibility in England, as later to the Beautiful
Soul, *die Schöne Seele*, in Germany, and finally to the
concept of Genius throughout Europe. In England it
was the custom to appeal to the authority of Milton's *Il*

Penseroso to fortify the belief that melancholy was a state of mind peculiarly favorable to moral elevation. Milton's poem is echoed in hundreds of eighteenth-century verses. Of course, Milton also wrote a companion poem on mirth, but if Milton allowed any moral elevation to mirth in that poem, the suggestion was overlooked by the eighteenth century.

However, there are many kinds of melancholy. It takes innumerable forms, depending on the ideas from which it originates. There is the gentle melancholy, which Thomas Gray expressed in his *Elegy*. There is the more superficial but charming and gay melancholy of Jaques in *As You Like It*, who cultivated his own sense of superiority by railing at the world. As the sharp-witted Rosalind told him, "Thou hast sold thy own lands to see others, and now thou hast nothing." But Jaques was not exactly to the taste of the eighteenth century; he was not sufficiently interested in virtue or the moral beauty of his soul. Among English poets of the eighteenth century Edward Young was given a peculiar eminence, due to a misreading of his work in England and a mistranslation of it into French. He was in reality a stern preacher, impressing on his readers the Christian doctrine that death is the inevitable end of all of us, that the soul after death will to all eternity be either saved or damned, and that we should seriously concern ourselves with preparation for death. It is difficult to see anything pleasurable in the contemplation of this human predicament, and Dr. Johnson for his part found it simply terrifying.

But when *Night Thoughts* was translated into languishing French or German poetic prose, it took its place beside Ossian in the highest rank of all European literature on the pleasures of melancholy.

Another form of melancholy outside of the true sentimental tradition is that of Gray's two early odes: *Ode on a Distant Prospect of Eton College* and the *Hymn to Adversity*. The Greek mottoes he prefixed to these poems express their spirit. From Aeschylus he quotes: "Zeus, who leads mortals to understanding, who has established as a fixed ordinance that wisdom comes to men by suffering." And from Menander: "I am a man; sufficient cause for being unhappy." The schoolboys of Eton, engaged in their childhood play, should be warned that they are men; they should be told, not that they are men and not boys, but that they are men and not gods:

> all are men,
> Condemned alike to groan,
> The tender for another's pain;
> Th'unfeeling for his own.

Adversity is supplicated as a divine power to teach the same lesson:

> Daughter of Jove, relentless Power,
> Thou tamer of the human breast,
> Whose iron scourge and tort'ring hour,
> The Bad affright, afflict the Best!

Such melancholy is not of the sweet and pleasurable kind. It is saved from bitterness by its resignation and humility, but it is a frank admission that human beings must accept life on the terms on which alone it is offered. It was Gray's *Hymn to Adversity* that inspired Wordsworth to write his *Ode to Duty*, a poem of courage and resolve. Gray's melancholy here is quite different from the later *Weltschmerz* of the century. It is worth noting that it was not these early odes, but *The Bard* and the poems from the Norse which, aside from the *Elegy*, interested the literati both in England and on the Continent.

We must also pass by the melancholia which is essentially a medical problem, such as Dr. Johnson suffered from, and which had been the subject of medical discussion from before Burton's *Anatomy of Melancholy* down to Dr. Cheyne's *The English Malady*. This affliction, as Dr. Johnson so well knew, was not conducive either to virtue or happiness. We come nearer to the subject of our investigation in Boswell's hypochondria, which, as Johnson brutally told him, he cherished and took pride in, and managed to reconcile with a life of agreeable sensations. In fact, Boswell's melancholy was itself one of the agreeable sensations. It was Boswell's kind of melancholy, of which the soul is capable only when it is to elegance refined, that fairly intoxicated the age. It was already a familiar phenomenon in European literature before Boswell was born. Sentimental drama in France and England, sentimental novels by Prévost and Richardson, poetry of nature and solitude, meditations on death and mutability, all of these were popular resources for cultivating divine melancholy. By 1745 a well defined cluster of themes had gathered around the theme of melancholy, and Thomas Warton, an intelligent, scholarly, and sensitive Oxford student, only seventeen years old, collected them into a poem on *The Pleasures of Melancholy*. As this poem in turn anticipated and stimulated later developments, it provides an excellent starting point for examining the peculiar cult of melancholy that distinguished the latter part of the eighteenth century.

Warton expressed an aversion to "Mirth's mad shouts"; "never," he begged, "let Euphrosyne beguile / With toys of wanton mirth my fixed mind." For in spite of all her attractiveness, "Yet are the joys that Melancholy gives, / By Contemplation taught, her sister sage, / Than all her witless revels happier far." Melancholy is therefore related to wisdom. But she is also to be valued because she gives us more "secret transports" and "loftier raptures" than the "solemn dullness of the tedious world." It is true that the shepherd on Hymettus can look down on the plain of Attica and the splendid beauty of Athens; but the musing hermit feels "truer joys" as he looks down on a different view, the ruined remains and "sunk magnificence" of Persepolis:

> a blended scene
> Of moles, fanes, arches, domes, and palaces,
> Where with his brother Horror, Ruin sits.

The tragedy of Eloisa is given a new turn by contrasting her with Cosmelia, the fashionable London lady who uses cosmetics, who floats "amid the gilded sons of dress" through the Mall "in silken pomp arrayed." For Eloisa, a devotee of the pleasures of melancholy, lives on a higher level; she,

> whose mind
> Had languished to the pangs of melting love,
> More secret transport found, as on some tomb
> Reclined she watched the tapers of the dead,
> Or through the pillared aisles, amid the shrines
> Of imaged saints, and intermingled graves, . . .
> Musing she wandered.

Melancholy is thoughtful, she loves to muse, and like her sister Contemplation she is sage. But Warton also warns us that these loftier raptures and sacred musings are not for men of coarser fibre. Only a "few know that elegance of soul refined / Whose soft sensation feels a quicker joy / From Melancholy's scenes." But such noble excellence of soul must be the desire of every man of nice feeling. It is not enough to be born qualified for it. He must strive for it and cultivate it. For, as I have already said, melancholy became a cult.

This peculiar melancholy of sensibility dominated European literature in the latter half of the eighteenth century. The widest reputations were won by its devotees. Perhaps the greatest of all was Rousseau, whom Byron, his disciple and admirer described as

> the self-torturing sophist, wild Rousseau,
> The apostle of affliction, he who threw
> Enchantment over passion, and from woe
> Wrung overwhelming eloquence.[3]

As Émile Faguet put it, Rousseau made the endowment

of tears into a kind of religious vocation.[4] But as we have already said something about Rousseau, let us pass him by here and examine the now nearly-forgotten Ossian.

In 1760, the year before Rousseau published his *Nouvelle Héloïse,* Macpherson gave to the world some fragments of poetic prose which he alleged were translated from the Gaelic of the fourth century. They caused an immediate sensation, and Macpherson was encouraged to add two short epic poems, *Fingal* and *Temora,* in 1762 and 1763. Doctor Blair, Regius Professor of Rhetoric and Belles-Lettres at Edinburgh, promptly published a *Critical Dissertation on the Poems of Ossian,* in which he brought his great learning to the aid of his fervent admiration of these poems. There were a few, like Dr. Johnson, who questioned the authenticity of the poems, and when Johnson was asked the clinching question, whether he thought any modern man could have written these poems, he replied, "yes, sir; many men, many women, and many children." As usual, poor Dr. Johnson was fighting on the losing side. For Ossianism burst like a storm over Europe. Already in 1760 the circle of Diderot in Paris discovered the greatness of the new poetry and Turgot published a translation of some of the fragments. Diderot himself admired them, Grimm compared them with Homer, and Suard with Pindar, the Prophets of the Old Testament, Homer, and Milton. All this in Paris in 1760. Germany soon joined the chorus of acclamation. Lessing and Klopstock were enthusiastic, and Herder compared Ossian to Moses and Job. From Italy

Cesarotti wrote Macpherson that Scotland has given the world a new Homer who never nods and who never babbles. In 1771 Goethe translated the *Song of Selma* for Frederike Brion, and he used the reading of this song to bring about the crisis in the story of Werther (1774). Werther, who was the image of Goethe himself at the beginning of the Storm and Stress period, the sorrowful Werther, records in his diary how he was converted to Ossian.

> Ossian has superseded Homer in my heart. To what a world does the illustrious bard carry me! To wander over pathless wilds, surrounded by impetuous whirlwinds, where, by the feeble light of the moon, we see the spirits of our ancestors; to hear from the mountain tops, mid the roar of the torrents, their plaintive sounds issuing from deep caverns, and the sorrowful lamentations of a maiden who sighs and expires on the mossy tomb of the warrior by whom she was adored. I meet this bard with silver hair; he wanders in the valley; he seeks the footsteps of his fathers, and, alas! he finds them only in their tombs. Then, contemplating the pale moon, as she sinks beneath the waves of the rolling seas, the hero remembers and sings of by gone days.

The melancholy Werther spoke indeed for all Germany, and all Europe, in this passionate longing for the wild, stormy, moon-lit, ghostly landscape and for the sad tales of long ago which fit so appropriately into the landscape.

We may observe parenthetically that Goethe changed his ideas during his long life, and in later years he rather depreciated his *Sorrows of Werther* as an unwholesome work. And in his old age, in a conversation with Eckermann, he remarked rather unkindly that when Werther read Ossian to Charlotte he was already on the verge of madness. But literary Europe did not drop Ossian as easily as Goethe did. Ossianism lasted well up to 1830 and left its mark on much of the literature of melancholy up to that time.

But there were other ideas that gained ascendancy at this time, largely because they were associated with Ossianism. The appearance of the Celtic Homer provided unexpected support for a new philosophy of history, of art, poetic genius, and of human nature in general.

Macpherson's publications came at a most opportune time, just when an enthusiastic antiquarianism was directing attention to the old Norse literature, and to the legends and myths of the old Germanic world. The revelation that the Caledonians of Scotland, in an age when they had not yet been touched by Christianity or the civilization of the Roman Empire, had in fact produced a poet of the stature of Homer, was so startling that it required a complete readjustment of history. These primitive barbarians of the North had equalled the Greeks; Ossian could supplant Homer. In the confusion of anthropological ignorance, every nation laid claim to being related to the Caledonians. The French, having some Celtic blood, as in Brittany, claimed Ossian as their own for that reason. The Germans and Swedes, believing that the Caledonians, as they were living so far North, were as Germanic as the Norsemen, regarded Ossian as a true Germanic possession. All of this misinformation assisted such men as Herder in formulating an antithesis between southern and northern European cultures, between the Latin and Germanic temperaments and traditions of art and literature. Even to our time we have the distinction between French and Latin opera on the one hand, and Wagnerian opera on the other. Ossianism contributed not a little to this emancipation of Germanic literature and culture and music from the long tyranny of Mediterranean classicism, or, to be less vague, from the tyranny of Paris. But this whole argument put a new emphasis on the nationalistic, even on the racial aspect of literature, of literature as something that must spring spontaneously from the peculiar characteristics and traditions of a people. Such a view lent a new significance and purpose, a new enthusiasm, to the study of all the old Germanic heritage, the old myths and legends, to Norse literature and the *Nibelungenlied*, and finally to *Beowulf* when the manuscript of it was at last discovered. And thus the way was prepared, not only for Wagner, but also for Tennyson's assurance that "dark and true and tender is the North."

It was noticed at once that the humanity presented in the Ossianic poems was dark and true and tender. Such sweet and gentle sensibility might of course have been expected in a people as primitive, as close to nature, as the Caledonians of the fourth century. But then again it was an age of barbarism, of continual wars and feuds and death in battle. And as Ossian was incessantly compared with Homer, and his heroes juxtaposed with Homeric heroes, it could not but be observed that the Caledonians were warriors with a difference; they were inexplicably humane; they fought and killed, but they lacked the barbaric gusto. They seemed to prefer gentle and mild moods, especially moods of tender sorrow and mournful lamentation. This fondness for sensibility was often pointed out, not only to prove that Ossian represented a higher humanity than Homer, but also that these Caledonians, the representatives of the North, had attained a higher ethical level than the Greeks, representatives of the Mediterranean nations. However, there were difficulties also with this theory, and Blair honestly noted them even before the theory had had time to get well established. We are not concerned with the fortunes of the theory, but with the light that Blair's comments throw on the nature of the Ossianic poems. For Blair pointed out that Ossian differs not only from Homer, but also from the old Gothic poetry of the North, which is as fierce and warlike as Homer and which also exalts bravery and contempt of death. The Gothic poetry of the North, said Blair,

> is such poetry as we might expect from a barbarous nation. It breathes a most ferocious spirit. It is wild, harsh, and irregular. . . . But when we open the works of Ossian, a very different scene presents itself. There we find the fire and enthusiasm of the most early times, combined with an

amazing degree of regularity and art. We find tenderness, and even delicacy of sentiment, greatly predominant over fierceness and barbarity. Our hearts are melted with the softest feelings, and at the same time elevated with the highest ideas of magnanimity, generosity, and true heroism. When we turn from the poetry of [the Danish king] Lodbrog to that of Ossian, it is like passing from a savage desert into a fertile field and cultivated country.

"How," asks Blair, "is this to be accounted for? or by what means to be reconciled with the remote antiquity attributed to these poems?"

Blair offers a suggestion. He thinks that there may have been a long tradition of a sort of college of bards which developed a great poetic style. That would account for the regularity and smoothness of style. But Blair, and many after him, could explain the moral beauty of this primitive people only as the fortunate result of their natural state, for in Ossian there is no mention of agriculture, handicrafts, business transactions, towns, or any economic problems. The life of the Caledonians had not been poisoned by civilization. Therefore they fought their battles only to correct injustices (though we interrupt to ask where the injustices came from); they were loyal and tender in love and friendship; their hearts melted at the sight of the unfortunate, and their legacy to posterity was this wonderful sweet lamentation accompanied by the winds over the sea and the tempest in the mountains. They expressed all the emotions of the

German *Sturm und Drang* literature, they had all the virtues of the man of feeling or the beautiful soul. We, after two hundred years of history, have of course no difficulty in explaining these aspects of Ossian. Macpherson, the author, was a young man of the eighteenth century, sensitive to all the various sentimental developments of his age, which naturally were reflected in his own compositions. The expression "joy in grief" frequently appears in the Ossianic poems. Blair tried to explain this phrase by noting a couple of Homeric parallels. But this will not do. The Ossianic joy in grief was the attraction that drew Werther *away* from Homer, and the judgment of the young German poets of the Storm and Stress period was surely that the melancholy of Ossian stirred them in a way that Homer's sadness did not. The sentimentalists of the eighteenth century were discriminating readers, and they knew that Ossian was of their kind and that Homer was not. Moreover, if they were poets, Ossian was the kind of bardic and inspired voice of nature that they also aspired to be.

The virtuous emotions, as we have seen, well up spontaneously from the depths of the man of sensibility. The eighteenth century developed in an analogous way a conception of the creative activity of true genius. For as virtue and genius were both excellences of human nature, they seemed to the eighteenth century to be closely related, and in men of great endowment almost one and the same. The idea of genius was of course ancient, and recognized by the Classical critics of modern times, such as Ben Jonson, Boileau, Dryden, Pope, and Addison. But the Classicists had always added the idea of craftsmanship to the idea of genius. By the middle of the eighteenth century there had developed a feeling that craftsmanship and literary tradition were injurious to native genius. The greatest poets of the past were spontaneous and natural, and more or less unhampered by education. Homer was greater than Virgil, Shakespeare greater than the learned Jonson. And now Ossian was nothing less natural than the storms that swept over his white hairs. Looking back to the Middle Ages with a fresh curiosity investigators were struck by such improvising poets as the Norse Skald, and even better, the Celtic Bard. Gray struck the right note in his Pindaric Ode *The Bard,* in which the Celtic poet is presented as a primitive and natural force, sublime and free as the storms of the Welsh mountains, and gifted even with prophetic powers. The *Geniezeit* liked to speak of the poet as a prophet, not quite literally, of course, but to indicate the enthusiastic and spontaneous vision which was the gift of the true genius, and it came to be assumed as the excellence of a profound and constitutional melancholy. That was something quite new. When Addison set forth his ideas on original genius in the *Spectator,* Number 160, he said nothing about melancholy. Even Edward Young, who however was a very old man when he published his *Conjectures on Original Composition* in 1759, even Edward Young, author of Night Thoughts, did not require that the original genius should be melancholy. But change was in the air. The fragments of Ossian appeared the very next year. James Beattie's popular poem *The Minstrel* was published in 1771. Beattie was Professor of Moral Philosophy at Aberdeen and his philosophical writings were sufficiently old-fashioned to win the approbation of Dr. Johnson. But in *The Minstrel* Beattie, who was only thirty-six years old, showed that he could respond to the new spirit then abroad. As he traced the progress of genius in a poet of humble birth, he not only attributed to him a capacity for self-education according to Nature, but he distinguished him from the mediocrity of the common herd by his natural retiring melancholy:

> Responsive to the sprightly pipe when all
> In sprightly dance the village-youth were join'd,
> Edwin, of melody aye held in thrall,
> From the rude gambol far remote reclined,
> Sooth'd with the soft notes warbling in the wind.
> Ah then, all jollity seem'd noise and folly;
> To the pure soul by Fancy's fire refined
> When with the charm compared of heavenly melancholy!

> Is there a heart that music cannot melt?
> Ah me! how is that rugged heart forlorn!
> Is there, who ne'er those mystic transports felt
> Of solitude and melancholy born?
> He needs not woo the Muse; he is her scorn.
> The sophist's rope of cobweb he shall twine;
> Mope o'er the schoolman's peevish page; or mourn,
> And delve for life, in Mammon's dirty mine;
> Sneak with the scoundrel fox, or grunt with glutton swine.

But there is nothing novel in Beattie's poem. This picture of the genius as the withdrawn or solitary enthusiast with a sensitive, melancholy, and ultimately tempestuous soul, was already in 1771 the common property of the sentimental movement all over Europe. There was no direct connection between Beattie in Scotland and Goethe in Germany. But Goethe's Werther lamented that life in a society of mediocre spirits, with their restrictive laws and decorum, can only be fatal to the free activity of the poet, which to ordinary people seems an uncontrollable and undesirable tempest. "O my friend," writes Werther,

> why is it that the torrent of genius so seldom bursts forth, so seldom rolls in full-flowing stream, overwhelming your astounded soul? Because, on either side of the stream, cold and respectable persons have taken up their abodes, and forsooth, their summer-houses and tulip-beds would suffer from the torrent; wherefore they dig trenches, and raise embankments betimes, in order to avert the impending danger.

Thus the late eighteenth century developed what modern social psychologists would call the image of the genius. The lonely and embittered Hamlet was assimilated into this image, and Goethe's interpretation of Hamlet in *Wilhelm Meister* is Shakespeare's character with Wertherism added. The age of the apotheosis is significantly also the age of *Weltschmerz;* and the genius cherished his cosmic pessimism as truly as Boswell cherished his melancholia, or the Ossianic poet his "joy in grief." For the suffering genius was very proud of his suffering, it was the badge and mark of his divine gift. Madame de Staël was a part of the age, as we shall see in a moment. But she had moments of remarkable insight when she could comment shrewdly on it. In her book on Germany she paused in one place to imagine herself in a position to have advised Rousseau regarding his melancholy and his persecution complex; she pays him every compliment, she appreciates his difficulties and sympathizes with his suffering, and yet she tells him that she fears he is proud over it all. She would counsel humility and resignation in a world full of evil; she would counsel prayer, for in prayer one is not alone in the universe; by such humility and resignation Madame de Staël thought the tempest in Rousseau's soul might be allayed and a gentle peacefulness restored to his life. Rousseau had been in his grave a quarter of a century when this imaginary conversation was published. And no contemporary geniuses seem to have taken any notice of this advice in *De L'Allemagne,* certainly not Byron, who was just then about to emerge as a popular poet and who aspired to be of all poets the most tempestuous, and who created in his own image a whole series of suffering and melancholy egoists.

We have commented on a text from Madame de Staël. But we must return to ideas which she held more consistently. No one spoke more eloquently than Madame de Staël about the untamed, stormy, original genius as the sublimest manifestation of human nature, soaring above us with an eagle's flight, subject to no laws but its own. The true poet is divine, he "improvises, in the manner of the sibyl and the prophets, the sacred hymns of genius." This enthusiasm and elevation of the mind is essential to the search for truth, even, she says, for abstract truth. It illuminates our faculties. It stirs our feeling for the good and the beautiful. It is the source of our truest happiness.

> Poetry and the fine arts serve to develop in man that happiness of exalted origin which lifts up again the hearts that are dejected, and which substitutes for the restless surfeit of life, that habitual sentiment of the divine harmony of which we and nature are parts. There is no duty, no pleasure, no sentiment to which enthusiasm does not lend I know not what enchantment, the harmony with the pure delight of truth.

Madame de Staël had already drawn the portrait of such a genius in her *Corinne,* a novel of Italy. And her visit to Germany seemed to her to reveal that here was a people naturally enthusiastic, fitted to produce a great sentimental literature. Her book on Germany has quite rightly been regarded as a manifesto of the Romantic Movement. Her temperament was predominantly sentimental, and even as she tried to expound Kant's conception of duty and conscience, it melted for her into mere feeling and sentiment.[5]

We have now come a long way from Milton and *Il*

Penseroso. The imagination recoils from the thought of drawing any comparison between the youthful John Milton and Ossian, the *Sorrows of Werther,* or eighteenth-century *Weltschmerz.* But we may draw some distinctions between the sentimental type of melancholy and similar moods in Gray and Johnson. Gray had his Ossianic enthusiasm, but, as we have seen, in his early odes he brooded over the sad destiny of man with a melancholy very different from the Ossianic. His was the melancholy of the chastened and humble heart,—just what Madame de Staël would have recommended to Rousseau,—and Gray beseeches Adversity, the daughter of Jove, to tame his heart and teach him resignation. As for Johnson, the sentimental enthusiasts would never have admitted him to their select circle. For all his melancholy temperament and his melancholy view of life, that poor man was never capable of those higher transports and sacred raptures which melancholy afforded to so many of his contemporaries. Moreover, he was obtuse to the merits of sentimental morality. He sternly refused to admit that these enthusiasms were really sources of moral insight or moral energy. He would not trust the conduct either of himself or of others to the guidance of mere inclinations of benevolence or mere feelings of sympathy for other people. Dr. Johnson, like Bishop Butler, insisted that the inclination to goodness needs the support of the idea of obligation involved in the moral judgment. Johnson remarked in his criticism of his friend Savage that the love of virtue, the enthusiasm over virtue, must not be accepted as a substitute for virtue itself. Johnson's statement is a strangely prophetic criticism of what was to come later in the century, of Rousseau and his "intoxication with virtue," of the whole sweeping movement of the next generations. The heart won the victory over the head. But Jonathan Swift had remarked long before that the human heart is a treasury of baseness and treachery and evil. When all its contents were released, strange elements came to join with the "joy in grief" of Ossian and the sorrows of Werther.

4

*The Culmination
in Horror*

MILTON'S companion poems, *L'Allegro* and *Il Penseroso*, are complementary in nature, not contradictory. They present two different conceptions of both mirth and melancholy. The "vain deluding joys, / The brood of Folly without father bred," which Milton orders away in *Il Penseroso* are of somewhat lower quality than the joys actually celebrated in *L'Allegro*. Likewise the pleasures of melancholy in the former poem are not what one would expect from the description of melancholy in the latter. It would have been most inappropriate, certainly, to have begun *Il Penseroso* with this invocation:

> Come heavenly melancholy,
> Of Cerberus and blackest Midnight born,
> In Stygian cave forlorn
> 'Mongst horrid shapes, and shrieks,
> and sights unholy.

There is no horror, no shrieking, nothing unholy in *Il Penseroso*. The bird of the night is sweet Philomel, most musical, most melancholy. But the eighteenth-century imitators of Milton made a strange alteration of this conception. They added to the melancholy of *Il Penseroso* those horrid shapes and shrieks and sights unholy that Milton had proscribed. They wooed the goddess Melancholy in different ways, in different haunts, the churchyard at midnight presenting itself to them at first as a very suitable place. To meet her, says Joseph Warton, in his *Ode to Fancy,*

> Let us with silent footsteps go,
> To charnels and the house of woe,
> To Gothic churches, vaults, and tombs. . . .

And Thomas Warton sought her beneath the moss-grown piles of a ruined abbey, Gothic of course, where sweet Philomel is replaced by the lone screech-owl. Walking there, says Thomas Warton,

> religious horror wraps
> My soul in dread repose.

By 1750 horror had already been added to the pleasures of melancholy, and the shrieks and sights unholy were not far off in the future. For the mid-eighteenth century marks the beginning of a period of literary exploitation of horror unprecedented in all previous history. Melancholy added new charms and new ways of charming. She moved from Gothic churches, preferably in ruins, with their charnels, to Gothic castles with secret passages and dungeons, the dark fastnesses of dark deeds, and thence to remote monasteries, also with secret subterranean dungeons, loathsome with vermin and fit only for the sadistic persecution and diabolical crimes which they hide from the light. For horror was at last sought, not only in these scenic backgrounds, but in the morbid developments possible to the human soul. To the other pleasures of melancholy were added the wild revels of a Walpurgis Night.

The writers of this literature, and also the modern scholars who have detailed its history, have generally used the words *terror* and *horror* without discriminating between them. But with all their common meaning, we all sense that they are not quite identical. It is possible to experience each without the other. According to Aristotle, tragedy purifies our emotions by inspiring in us pity and terror. In this context the correct word is *terror*, because terror is an apprehension of something that may happen in the future, and as we watch the tragic hero involving himself, usually unwittingly or thoughtlessly, in a mesh that will lead to his own destruction, we sit in sympathetic fear for him, we would like to warn him, as Kent warns Lear not to indulge in "this hideous rashness." Such is the terror joined with pity in the true tragic vision. The catastrophes of great tragedy are not usually horrible, even though the stage may be strewn with corpses as at the end of *Hamlet*. A scene of horror before the final curtain would obviously make impossible the experience which we refer to as catharsis, the exaltation of mind which is the mysterious effect of great tragedy. But horror may be inspired by something past or present as well as by something apprehended in the future. It may be combined with terror, but it need not be. Burke thought that Virgil seemed to be seized "with a religious horror" as he was about to unfold in the *Aeneid* the secrets of the waste and dark dominions of Hades.[1] It would not be difficult to make a long list of scenes or situations or objects which we would call horrible even though they threaten no danger to the spectator who regards them with horror. We might distinguish roughly between our reactions by saying that the terrible makes us tremble whereas the horrible makes us shudder. It is a shudder that Beattie wished to excite in us as he tells of the dreams of his young genius wandering at night in the lonely vale.

> There would he dream of graves, and corses pale;
> And ghosts, that to the charnel-dungeon throng,
> And drag a length of clanking chain, and wail,
> Till silenced by the owl's terrific song,
> Or blast that shrieks by fits the shuddering aisles along.

Readers in the eighteenth century probably shuddered more over these lines than we do, but even so it must have been one of the milder shudders of the period. However, these mild shudders became so common in poetry that already in 1763 they invited parody. Someone in that year compiled a recipe for "a gentleman who desired proper materials for a monody," that is, a dirge; the poem is an enumeration of the best materials then in use:

> Flowrets—wreaths—thy banks along—
> Silent eve—th' accustomed song—
> Black-browed night—Hark! screech-owls sing!
> Ebon car—and raven wing—
> Charnel houses—lonely dells—
> Glimmering tapers—dismal cells—
> Hallow'd haunts—and horrid piles—
> Roseate hues—and ghastly smiles—
> Solemn fanes—and cypress bowers—

Thunder — storms — and tumbling towers —
   Let these be well together blended —
Dodsley's your man — the poem's ended.[2]

But the shudders in such poems have not yet quite
reached the point of morbidity. They can give us all the
pleasure of a mild thrill. The mild thrill has a certain
value. It was only a few years earlier than this parody,
in 1757, that Burke had published his *Philosophical In-
quiry into the Origin of our Ideas on the Sublime and
Beautiful,* in which he advanced the theory that an element of pain or terror is a necessary ingredient in our
experience of the sublime. And Burke did not distinguish
between horror and terror. For instance, he says that
after our escape from danger we experience, "not pleasure, but a sort of delightful horror, a sort of tranquillity
tinged with terror."[3] In another place he says that we
find our minds "in a state of much sobriety, impressed
with a sense of awe, in a sort of tranquillity shadowed
with horror." Burke's descriptions seem indeed to ap-
proximate the experience of catharsis in great tragedy.
And it is true that some of the later writers of horror literature were aware of Burke's theory of the sublime and
were more or less impressed by it. We may therefore
have occasion to recur to the sentences we have just
quoted from Burke, and use them as touchstones to test
the quality of some horrors we are about to contemplate.

The parody just quoted of the mild funeral dirges
appeared in 1763. Only two years later Horace Walpole
gave a powerful new impetus to horror literature with

The Castle of Otranto, which made even Thomas Gray afraid to go to bed. This incredible melodrama no longer frightens modern readers, who have much more powerful stimuli at their disposal. But in 1765, and for a long time thereafter, readers could not escape from the spell of this vast and gloomy medieval structure, with its subterranean passages and vaults, mysterious and sinister, awesome in their dark silence. Now and then some blasts of wind shook the doors which grated on the rusty hinges, and the noises were re-echoed through the long labyrinth of darkness. No wonder the heroine, trying to find her way to safety through these passages to the altar of the chapel, was struck with a new terror at every murmur and felt her blood curdle when she thought she heard the footstep of some human being. She had been saved from a forced marriage to the son of Manfred, the tyrant of the castle, by nothing less than the mysterious fall of an enormous helmet which killed the groom on his way to the ceremony. But this was only the first of a series of blood-curdling incidents. A portrait of Manfred's grandfather was hanging in the hall; it stepped out of the frame, motioned to Manfred to follow, and then disappeared from him behind a mysteriously closed door. A statue in the hall bled at the nose. Manfred was, of course, deep in criminal designs, and he murdered his own daughter by mistake, though his evil designs on the heroine were averted. In the final scene a clap of thunder shook the castle to its foundations, and the spirit of Theodore, the true heir to the castle, appeared. After the walls of the castle were thrown down by some mighty force, the spirit of Theodore revealed his secret, whatever it was, and then, accompanied by a clap of thunder, ascended solemnly toward heaven, where, the clouds having parted asunder, the form of St. Nicholas could be seen receiving Theodore, and then they were both wrapt from mortal eyes in a blaze of glory. It should be added that this supernatural spectacle was sufficient to bring Manfred to a state of penitence, and he took on him the habit of religion in a neighboring convent. After the horrors we have witnessed, this tame conclusion comes as an anticlimax. It would have been worth something to have had Satan carry Manfred off to hell. But this was only 1765. Before the end of the century authors will give us plenty of criminals who are mysteriously incapable of repentance.

Walpole's little romance was immediately popular, but as historians point out, it was thirty years later that the novel of terror really came into its own. The current fiction writers must have found the eccentric sensationalism of *The Castle of Otranto* difficult to digest for their own purposes, and we know at any rate that they were for the moment concentrating on other pursuits. They were busy providing a profusion of novels of sensibility for the new circulating libraries, whence the Lydia Languishes of the time borrowed them, with or without their parents' consent. These novels were of course in the school of Richardson, but with the addition of various English and French innovations, and later of German elements. A young Scot, Henry Mackenzie, published in 1771 a noteworthy little novelette called *The Man of Feeling*, which immediately became a sort of classic of the sentimental movement. He later added more pretentious novels, and in 1785, in his essay periodical *The Lounger*, he continued with some very pretty little tales of sensibility. He should therefore be an authority on the novel of sensibility. It is very interesting that in *The Lounger*, Number 20, he should also issue a warning against the dangers of these novels, though we must presume that he is excepting his own:

> The principal danger of Novels, as forming a mistaken and pernicious system of morality, seems to me to arise from that contrast between one virtue and another, that war of duties which is to be found in many of them, particularly in that species called the *Sentimental*. . . . In the enthusiasm of sentiment there is much the same danger as in the enthusiasm of religion, of substituting certain impulses and feelings of what may be called the visionary kind, in the place of real practical duties, which in morals, as in theology, we might not improperly denominate *good works*. In morals, as in religion, there are not wanting instances of refined sentimentalists, who are contented with talking of virtues which they never practise, who pay in words what they owe in actions; or perhaps, what is fully as dangerous, who open their minds to *impressions* which never have any effect upon their *conduct*, but are considered as something foreign to and distinct from it. This

separation of conscience from feeling is a depravity of the most pernicious sort; it eludes the strongest obligation to rectitude, it blunts the strongest incitement to virtue; when the ties of the first bind the sentiment and not the will, and the rewards of the latter crown not the heart but the imagination.

Mackenzie gave no specific examples of such perversion, but he may have had in mind, among other things, the young girls who were so inflamed by these novels that they spurned weddings and church ceremonies and longed ardently for the raptures of abduction and elopement. But we are mainly concerned to learn from so proficient a novelist of sensibility as Mackenzie that there was going on a dissociation of conscience from sentiment, and that the excitement of sensibility was being cultivated for its own sake regardless of consequences.

This development was taking place in spite of the professed moral purpose of the novelists. Dr. Johnson said of his friend Richardson's novels that they taught the passions to move at the command of virtue. Although many readers doubtless read and enjoyed them for other than moral reasons, it was certainly the purpose of Richardson to sustain the rights of morality as he understood them. But Richardson could not control the future. And already when he was writing, and even before, French novelists had made lewd engraftments on the novel of sensibility far more insidiously dangerous to morals than Fielding's *Joseph Andrews*, which wounded the pride as well as the moral feelings of Richardson. And the most influential of these foreigners was doubtless the Abbé Prévost, the very man who was later to translate Richardson's novels into French. Prévost's famous novels were written between 1728 and 1740, and were translated into English. And in these novels the historians of fiction have discovered some of the significant patterns for the later Gothic novel of terror. The most famous of them, *Cleveland*, will serve as an illustration. Cleveland is an English boy, the natural son of Oliver Cromwell, who in this novel not only had illegitimate children, but sought by criminal means to be rid of them. Cleveland and his mother take refuge in a vast cave called Romney Hole, where he grows up pretty much according to nature, and in due time falls in love with Fanny, the daughter of the Earl of Axminster, who also lived in the cave as a refugee from Cromwell's cruelty. After the mother dies and is buried in the cave, the Earl and Fanny and Cleveland manage to escape to France, and the calamities begin to fall on Cleveland, one after another, to the end of the long rambling story. They drift to Jamaica, where Fanny is carried away by an amorous sea captain. Cleveland pursues them to America, finds Fanny and her father naked in the woods, becomes a leader of a tribe of noble savages, whereupon they suffer first from a ravaging plague and then from an attack by a hostile tribe of Indians. Fanny, to whom Cleveland has by now been joined in marriage, is carried off by the hostile tribe and Cleveland thinks he sees her being burned alive. He is sold as a slave to the Spaniards, is released, returns to France, and after a number of years falls in love with a young girl who returns his love passionately. It is discovered just in time that she is his own lost daughter Cecile. Fanny is also discovered in a convent, her apparent death by burning being explained now as a misapprehension. Cecile dies from smallpox. Cleveland and Fanny return to England to end the story.

But this is only the bare thread on which the many episodes of calamities and sufferings are strung. And these episodes are the real jewels. Danger after danger threatens our hero, and grief is heaped on grief. Cleveland is the victim of Fate. "My name," he cries, "was written in the blackest, most fatal page in the book of destiny." This is his constant theme. In the English translation published in 1734–35, in the second volume, we read on page 237: "I was the sport of that malicious power which doomed me to be unhappy from my birth." Twenty pages later: "Life, in the manner it was granted me, was not so much a favour, as a fatal and poisonous gift." And so on. The sentimental movement was especially fond of the pathos of unmerited and accidental suffering, and Cleveland remarks in characteristic fashion that his wife was "fated to make me wretched, but undesignedly; and I, to be unhappy, without meriting to be so."

If the story of misfortune and calamity told in this manner falls lamentably short of the tragic catharsis, it has an appeal of its own,—the luxury of grief, that joy in grief which we have seen in Ossian and elsewhere. Even Cleveland explains that the manifestations of joy and grief are remarkably similar. And, he says, "if one man is transported with joy and the other with sorrow, I know not which of the two would be the more reluctant to be bereaved of the sensation he feels."[4] For the heart of the man of misery dotes on its sorrow as truly as the human heart does on its pleasures.[5] The hero of Prévost's novel *The Man of Quality* insists that sighs and griefs "have infinite sweetness for a person in mortal affliction. The moments that I devoted to my grief were so dear to me that to prolong them I abstained from sleep."[6] There are compensations, it seems, for living in a malign and ominous world,—at any rate, there are pleasures in reading about it. Thus the emotional pattern of the novels of Prévost before 1740 anticipated the luxurious melancholy and the thrill of impending horrors and catastrophes, states of mind quite necessary to get the excitement of the mysteries of the novel of terror. We observe also this early in the century an anticipation of the *Weltschmerz* which was the joy of the later generations, the pathetic helplessness of the good man or the beautiful soul in the toils, not of sin, but of cold and malign fate, the sorrowful suffering of Wertherism. And we have already more than a premonition of some moral confusions which appear with the later less restrained treatments of terror.

In the light of history it appears that the novel of terror was only a variant of the novel of sensibility, exploiting a fresh excitement, trying to push suspense and apprehension to the utmost. But devices for suspense tend to pall on repetition, and therefore new devices must be introduced, stimuli must be intensified, the voltage must be continually increased, so as to overcome the resistance of the reader. The supernatural was at first a useful resource, but as even ghosts can become commonplace, it was necessary to make them ghastly. Death and the grave could in time be contemplated with comparative tranquillity, whereupon it would be requisite to open the grave and expose the corrupting corpse with the worms. The bones that Thomas Warton and others contemplated piled neatly in the charnel could arouse only a feeble interest compared with the complete skeletons, active and grinning and sinister, which were later to pursue their horror-stricken victims. All this progress in England was not without substantial assistance from the German drama and novel and ballad. But then again the Germans professed to be disciples of the English. All the literary genres were marching forward on a regimental front to conquer both England and Germany for the sentimental movement. The German plays of the Storm and Stress period, Goethe's *Götz von Berlichingen* and Schiller's *The Robbers*, with their noble but rude and defiant heroes, were followed by the sensational and fourth-rate plays of Kotzebue, and all were imported into England and became the popular theatrical fare. In his *Biographia Literaria* Coleridge recorded his opinion as to both the origin and the literary value of this German importation. We have only to combine, he thought, the styles of English authors then popular in German to find all the elements of it:

> the bloated style and peculiar rhythm [of Hervey's *Meditations*] . . . the strained thoughts, the figurative metaphysics, and solemn epigrams of Young . . . the loaded sensibility, the minute detail, the morbid consciouness of every thought and feeling in the whole flux and reflux of the mind, in short the self-involution and dream-like continuity of Richardson . . . then to add the horrific incidents, the mysterious villains, . . . the ruined castles, the dungeons, the trap-doors, the skeletons, the flesh-and-blood ghosts, and the perpetual moonshine of a modern author (themselves the literary brood of the *Castle of Otranto* . . .), and, as the compound of these ingredients duly mixed, you will recognize the so-called *German* drama.

It is therefore, concludes Coleridge, "*English* in its *origin, English* in its *materials,* and *English* by re-adoption."[7]

In our limited time we can examine only an illustration of these international convolutions of the techniques and motifs of the literature of terror by observing the transformations of the old ballad of Fair Margaret and Sweet William. It was popularized in a modernization by David Mallet, at least as early as 1724. In this version the ghost of Margaret comes from her grave to visit at night her faithless lover, whose betrayal has caused her death. The ghost ends her plaint with some very plain-spoken words:

> That face, alas! no more is fair;
>   Those lips no longer red;
> Dark are my eyes, now closed in death,
>   And every charm is fled.
>
> The hungry worm my sister is;
>   This winding-sheet I wear;
> And cold and weary lasts our night,
>   Till that last morn appear.
>
> But hark! — the cock has warned me hence;
>   A long and late adieu!
> Come, see, false man, how low she lies,
>   Who died for love of you.
>
> The lark sang loud; the morning smil'd,
>   With beams of rosy red;
> Pale William quak'd in every limb,
>   And raving left his bed.
>
> He hied him to the fatal place
>   Where Margaret's body lay;
> And stretch'd him on the grass-green turf,
>   That wrapp'd her breathless clay.
>
> And thrice he called on Margaret's name,
>   And thrice he wept full sore;
> Then laid his cheek to her cold grave,
>   And word spake never more!

Just fifty years later Bürger, an erratic young genius of the Göttingen school, achieved immortality with one poem, the ballad called *Lenore,* inspired by the William and Margaret ballads of England. But he chose another variant of the story, a ballad called *Sweet William's Ghost,* in which the situation is reversed, and it is William who comes to claim the fickle Margaret in a marriage of death. In Bürger's ballad the spectre of William carries Lenore on a wild and grisly night-ride to the side of his grave, his bride in death. The sensation of this poem was immense. In the year 1796 four different English translations of it appeared, as well as two imitations by Walter Scott. But it remained for "Monk" Lewis to exhaust, as it would seem, the possibilities of horror in such a narrative in his ballad of *Alonzo the Brave and the Fair Imogene.* Lewis follows the same version as Bürger. The spectre of Alonzo appears at the wedding of the faithless Imogene and carries her off while all the wedding guests are paralyzed by fear, the dogs howl, and the tapers burn blue. After reprimanding her at the grave the spectre

> Then sank with his prey through the wide-yawning
> ground:
> Nor ever again was fair Imogene found,
> Or the spectre who bore her away.

But the Castle remains haunted regularly:

> At midnight four times in each year does her sprite,
> When mortals in slumber are bound,
> Arrayed in her bridal apparel of white,
> Appear in the hall with the Skeleton-Knight,
> And shriek as he whirls her around.

92

While they drink out of skulls newly torn from the
  grave,
  Dancing round them pale spectres are seen:
Their liquor is blood, and this horrible stave
They howl: "To the health of Alonzo the Brave,
  And his consort, the False Imogene!

We can all enjoy shuddering at this sort of thing,
especially as we need not take it very seriously. But we
are obviously far from the terror of the tragic view of
life, and also far from the terror that Burke associated
with the sublime. In his ballad Lewis is stirring that
latent appetite for the morbid which is in all of us, and
in his novel *The Monk* he indulged it to repletion. The
Madrid monastery which he chose as setting for his novel
was merely in outward appearance as gloomy and sinister as any haunted castle in earlier Gothic novels. It
was not conducive to that sobriety or tranquillity of mind
of which Burke had spoken. It suggested only secret
and hair-raising crime, evil shrouded in mystery; it was
the natural haunt of ghosts, perhaps even of fiends. Horror brooded over it. But as the story takes us into the subterranean caverns, in which so many of the crucial episodes of the story take place, we are shocked by scenes
more repulsive than anything previously described in
novels of terror. We see only a flickering grave-lamp
throw its faint rays through the dark vaults. Deeper there
are secret dungeons whose entrances are cunningly con-
cealed until the necessities of the narrative open them,
where we may discover some fallen nun or other cap-

tive chained to the wall, doomed to end a horrible existence in that awful loneliness. Here we may glimpse a human head of a victim, with worms devouring the putrescent flesh. A guilty nun, chained to her death, watches the worms, which have been devouring the rotting corpse of her child on the stone pavement before her, come crawling up and coiling around her own fingers. Such thrills the readers of sensibility were now able to enjoy.

But this is only the setting, appropriate and even necessary, for the story of the monk. When we first meet Ambrosio he is the popular preacher of Madrid, reputed a saint, and the glory not only of his monastery but of the Catholic Church. But Lucifer discovers that the weakness of the monk is his pride and sets out to destroy him. Sensation follows sensation in a crescendo of horror. Matilda, a beautiful but demonic woman, dresses as a boy, enters the monastery as a novitiate, and seduces Ambrosio. Thus started on a career of secret depravity, Ambrosio goes on to murder his mother and seduce his sister. When he is caught in the net of the Inquisition and is facing death in an *auto-da-fé,* he sells his soul to Lucifer for a promise to release him from prison. But Ambrosio, though he escaped from the Inquisition, finds that he is still the prey of Lucifer. When in the last scene he asks the fiend to take him to Matilda, the ferocious spirit informs him that Matilda is already in the flames of hell, where Ambrosio is now about to join her. He explains to the monk that the Antonia whom he had violated was his own sister, that the Elvira whom he had murdered was his own mother. Ambrosio, the former saint, raises his hands to heaven for help, but the fiend darts at him a look of fury, tells him his time for pardon was past, and exclaims: "Thus I secure my prey."

> As he said this, darting his talons into the monk's shaven crown, he sprang with him from the rock. The caves and mountains rang with Ambrosio's shrieks. The demon continued to soar aloft, till reaching a dreadful height, he released the sufferer. Headlong fell the monk through the airy waste: the sharp point of rock received him, and he rolled from precipice to precipice, till, bruised and mangled, he rested on the river's banks.

This attempt at a grandiose conclusion may seem to us a little flat and amateurish, but we must recognize the high literary value attributed to shrieks and mangled human flesh. As this novel was published in 1796 we may consider it significant as illustrating the literature of horror in mid-career. It had predecessors and successors. It is at once a summation of the previous Gothic romance in England, the *Schauerroman* of Germany, the Faust legend, the supernatural in the ballad, novel, and drama, and a prefiguration of future developments. It signalizes the impending exploitation of the demonic in literature, not merely in the audacious use of the supernatural, but specifically in the cultivation of the Satanic as a thrill. We may recall that it was at this very time that Milton's

Satan was in various quarters championed as the real hero of *Paradise Lost,* and that Milton was understood, as Blake said, to have been of the Devil's party without knowing it. As might be expected, the cult of *das dämonische* in human nature merged with all kinds of revolutionary feelings. And in its search for awe-inspiring and terrifying manifestations of human nature, this literature developed and exploited a type of noble criminal, lonely and brooding, splendid and yet dangerous, mysterious and unpredictable, an outlaw, not only from society, but from morality itself. Such a hero might be a revolutionist in this age of revolutionary thought, he might seem to be allied with good forces against the evils of the world, but he could at the same time be evil himself. He is the romantic criminal as hero, representing a sort of transvaluation of values. His main features appear already in Manfred, the violent, gloomy, mysterious tyrant in *The Castle of Otranto.* In later Gothic novels he continues to be the main source of the excitement and suspense, as his malevolent and unsearchable will spreads terror all about him. But this type of hero reached his greatest potency over the imagination, stimulated the greatest horror, when he was revealed as Satanic in nature. Then we find him exhibiting fiendish pleasure in cruelty, defiantly throwing off the bonds of humanity, cherishing the terrible secret of his unpardonable guilt, and facing heroically his inevitable damnation. Such a character exercises an hypnotic fascination over all of us. For of all the thrilling experiences possible to human nature, what can be more exciting than the experience of hell?

All the heroes of this type give us the pleasure of horror, a mixture of awe, admiration, and terror. They drink deep of life,—more deeply than we dare, and we are fascinated by their heroic and perilous experience. Through them we may eat of the forbidden fruit; we may explore the abnormal, the sinister, the horrible potentialities of human nature. We cannot but admire them for their strength and stature, as of Satan himself, and their scorn for that moral world from which we punier souls are incapable of extricating ourselves. As scholars have pointed out, from the literature of horror came the Byronic hero. Quite appropriately, Byron acknowledged that his drama of *Werner* was a dramatization of a Gothic novel by Harriet Lee. But the same theme recurs throughout Byron; not only in *Childe Harold,* and the dramas *Cain* and *Manfred,* but even in his early narrative poems we find these strong, heroic, mysteriously guilty men who are unable to repent. Byron himself thus describes his hero in *The Corsair:*

> There is a war, a chaos of the mind,
> When all its elements convulsed, combined,
> Lie dark and jarring with perturbed force,
> And gnashing with impenitent remorse; . . .
> Vain voice! the spirit burning, but unbent,
> May writhe, rebel—the weak alone repent.

This Byronic mood is not merely personal with Byron; it represents the whole *Weltschmerz* of the period, which

97

we have seen in Ossianic melancholy, the proud cherishing of suffering, now accentuated by impenitent guilt, and the defiance of moral health, which satisfied the secret craving for the strangeness of the horrors of the human soul.

These so-called Byronic heroes who appeared in all European literatures as the result of the general and common drift of thought and sensibility in all countries, are not difficult to analyze. Psychologically they are creatures of passion; philosophically they are the self-pitying victims of destiny. The passions of these powerful figures were always raging tempests within them, and to control or regulate these natural urges seemed to them and to their creators to be the first and deepest sin against the spirit of life itself. Byron's Giaour speaks for them all:

> I'd rather be the thing that crawls
> Most noxious o'er a dungeon's walls,
> Than pass my dull, unvarying days,
> Condemned to meditate and gaze. . . .
> The cold in clime are cold in blood,
>   Their love can scarce deserve the name;
> But mine was like a lava flood
>   That boils in Aetna's breast of flame.[8]

Such heroes are profound individualists, profound revolutionists in the moral realm, defiantly proclaiming their own integrity even in their crimes, and standing up in judgment, not upon themselves, but upon destiny, the universe, and whatever God there is. Like Faust, they want to live dangerously, to experience all the possibilities of human life, but with an inward assurance and expectation that, if they resolutely continue striving, the Spirit of Life will never permit Mephistopheles to snatch them away to eternal darkness. The criminal as hero was not new to literature, but in the literature of terror we have the old theme with a different ethos. Macbeth was a criminal and also a tragic figure. He had also explored the possibilities of *Menschlichkeit*, but we cannot imagine for him a sequel, a *Macbeth, Part Two*, like the second part of *Faust*. For we have seen Macbeth's gradual moral disintegration laid bare. For him there could be no second chance, such as Goethe gave to Faust. It would be absurd to imagine Macbeth awakening on a flowery turf, visited by lovely little spirits who sing to him that they are always ready with help:

> Be he holy, be he vicious,
> Pity they the luckless man.

> Ob er heilig, ob er böse,
> Jammert sie der Unglücksmann.

Shakespeare could not have imagined elves reviving Macbeth as they revive Faust:

> Thou art whole; let faith restore thee!
> Trust the new, the rising Day!

Macbeth could not have risen again to resume his vigorous pursuit of that highest life for which his soul was panting. *Macbeth* and *Faust* present two different worlds. *Faust* is the expression of the Romantic uncritical longing for experience and more experience, with the belief, as Santayana has said, that the universe is as wayward as itself. It ignores, to quote Santayana again, that "only in reference to what is not life—to objects, ideals, and unanimities that cannot be experienced but may only be conceived—can life become truly rational and truly progressive."[9]

Here we must stop in our experimental observation of the behavior of the human soul. What can we say in conclusion? First, we must admit that our experiment has been extremely limited, as all scientific investigations should be. We have traced only one line of development of sensibility. We have said nothing about the great philanthropic spirit of the eighteeth century, which had beneficent results lasting down to our own day. We have not noticed that terror-romanticism did not always cross the line into the morbid, that Sir Walter Scott, for instance, kept it under both moral and artistic control. Many other pertinent matters we have had to pass by. But we have been able to observe, I trust, how ethical theory, in its search for the true inwardness of the good life, dropped out the indispensable element of obligation, the moral judgment, and how it came to put all its trust in feelings, assuming that human nature is one and whole and good. This choice and propensity had a decisive influence on European thought and feeling for generations, and even to the present moment in our own country. We have seen a few beginnings of that gathering of the flowers of evil, of which any one may find a more copious collection in the volume published by Mario Praz thirty years ago, and which is available in English under the title *The Romantic Agony*. I do not suppose that this rather terrifying anthology of Satanism proves that we are all children of Satan and that Hell is our natural abiding place. But the natural history of the man of feeling may well make us pause and reflect about the constitution of our human nature. For the man of feeling surely had a noble ancestry, a noble upbringing, and, like Shelley, he was sure that he acted always from the highest motives. And yet, as he abandoned himself to what he thought was his complete humanity, his *Menschlichkeit*, he became susceptible to all those spiritual diseases which come under the category of *mal du siècle*, and that is how he came to crave and enjoy the horrible and the morbid. So Shelley gazed upon Leonardo's painting of the Medusa's head with its "tempestuous loveliness of terror" and pronounced that "its horror and its beauty are divine." Perhaps the following of this historical evolution can not only throw some scientific light on our common human nature, but as a spectacle inspire in us a kind of tranquil horror. Perhaps this episode of history may even give us an experience approaching the true tragic catharsis.

References

CHAPTER 1

1. *The Cambridge Platonists,* ed. E. T. Campagnac (Oxford, 1901), pp. 25, 43, 46.
2. Henry More, *Enchiridion Ethicum,* Facsimile Text Society (New York, 1930), p. 242.
3. *The Cambridge Platonists,* p. 55.
4. Shaftesbury, *Characteristics,* ed. J. M. Robertson (London, 1900), I, 53; II, 255.
5. Lois Whitney, *Primitivism and the Idea of Progress* (Baltimore, 1934), p. 32.
6. *Characteristics,* I, 81, 86, 305; II, 265, 267–69.
7. Bernard Mandeville, *Fable of the Bees,* ed. F. B. Kaye (Oxford, 1924), I, 51, 323.
8. Joseph Butler, *Fifteen Sermons,* in *Works,* ed. W. E. Gladstone (Oxford, 1896), II, 64.
9. Leslie Stephen, *History of English Thought in the Eighteenth Century* (New York, 1949), II, 74–75.
10. James Bonar, *Moral Sense* (London, 1930), p. 223.
11. Basil Willey, *The Eighteenth Century Background* (London, 1940), pp. 119–20.

12. David Hume, *Treatise on Human Nature*, Book III, Part I, and Part II, sec. i.

13. Rousseau, *Confessions*, Book IX.

14. Rousseau, *La Profession de foi du vicaire savoyard*, ed. P. M. Masson (Paris, 1914), pp. 265, 273.

15. Rousseau, *La Nouvelle Héloïse*, Part VI, letter vii.

16. Mme. de Staël, *De la littérature: Discours préliminaire*.

17. Friedrich Schiller, *Essays Æsthetical and Philosophical*, English translation (Bohn Library, 1916), pp. 199, 202.

CHAPTER 2

1. Daniel Mornet, *Diderot* (Paris, 1941), p. 53.

2. Diderot, *Œuvres*, ed. J. Assézat and M. Tourneux (Paris, 1875–77), VI, 315.

3. *Ibid.*, XIX, 448.

4. Diderot, *Supplément*, ed. Gilbert Chinard (Paris, 1935), pp. 190–91.

5. Letter to Sophie Volland, July 31, 1762.

6. *Œuvres*, III, 313–14.

7. Maurice Tourneux, *Diderot et Catherine II* (Paris, 1899), II, 323.

8. *Œuvres*, IX, 352.

9. "Salon de 1765," *Œuvres*, X, 251.

10. Letter to Sophie Volland, July 31, 1762.

11. *Œuvres*, VII, 127.

CHAPTER 3

1. James Thomson, *Spring*, I, 351.
2. *Summer,* II, 1379–83.
3. Byron, *Childe Harold's Pilgrimage,* III, 77.
4. Émile Faguet, *Le Dix-Huitième Siècle* (Paris, 1890), p. 421.
5. Mme. de Staël, *De L'Allemagne,* Part II, chap. x; Part IV, chaps. x–xii; Part III, chap. vi.

CHAPTER 4

1. Edmund Burke, *The Sublime and Beautiful,* Part II, sec. vi.
2. Eleanor M. Sickels, *The Gloomy Egoist* (New York, 1932), pp. 67 and 359.
3. *The Sublime and Beautiful,* Part IV, sec. vii.
4. Abbé Prévost, *The Life and Adventures of Mr. Cleveland,* English translation (London, 1734–35), III, 113; III, 82–83.
5. Paul Hazard, *Études Critiques sur "Manon Lascaut"* (Chicago, 1929), p. 43.
6. Ernest A. Baker, *History of the English Novel,* V (London, 1934), 126.
7. S. T. Coleridge, *Biographia Literaria,* ed. J. Shawcross (Oxford, 1907), II, 183–84.
8. Byron, *The Giaour,* II, 990–93 and 1099–1102.
9. George Santayana, *Three Philosophical Poets* (Cambridge, Mass., 1910), p. 199.

The manuscript was edited by Barbara Woodward. The book was designed by William A. Bostick using Linotype Caledonia designed by W. A. Dwiggins in 1939 for the text and News Gothic designed by Morris F. Benton for American Typefounders in 1908 for the display.

The book is printed by offset on Warren's 1854 text, regular finish. The binding for the hardcover edition is Joanna Mills' Parchment, linen finished, and the paper cover is Warren's Lustro Gloss Cover. Manufactured in the United States of America.